W9-BOA-180

JOHN WOOLMAN

•The MMCo•

A JOURNAL

OF THE

LIFE, GOSPEL LABORS, AND CHRISTIAN EXPERIENCES
OF THAT FAITHFUL MINISTER OF
JESUS CHRIST

JOHN WOOLMAN

TO WHICH ARE ADDED

His Last Epistle and Other Writings

The work of righteousness shall be peace; and the effect of righteousness, quietness and assurance for ever.

ISAIAH xxxii. 17.

New York
THE MACMILLAN COMPANY
LONDON: MACMILLAN & CO., LTD.
1910

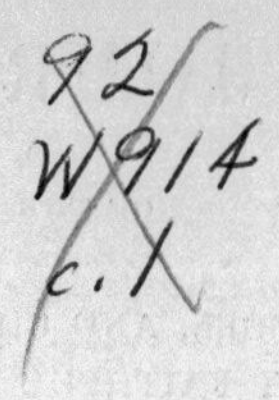

Set up and electrotyped. Published January, 1903. Reprinted January, 1910.

Norwood Press
J. S. Cushing Co. — Berwick & Smith Co.
Norwood, Mass., U.S.A.

CONTENTS

CHAPTER III

CHAPTER IV

CHAPTER V

INTRODUCTION

"We are taught by renewed experience to labor for an inward stillness; at no time to seek for words, but live in the spirit of truth, and utter that to the people which truth opened in us." These words disclose the secret of John Woolman's character and the charm of his Journal — a charm felt by those English writers and readers especially who were unusually sensitive to the finer qualities of style. No man has yet appeared on this side the Atlantic who has possessed in larger measure that inward repose which is free alike from the disturbances of the egotistic temperament and from the agitations of one whose aims are external and material. Woolman's aims were wholly impersonal; he seems to have been entirely free from ambition of any kind, and entirely absorbed in the pursuit of peace by the way of complete harmony with the divine will. That harmony he sought not only by self-surrender, but by active pursuit of righteousness. He was one of the most ardent antislavery men in those early days when the abolitionist was still in the distant future, and his gentleness gave his advocacy of the cause of the slave a persuasiveness denied most of his fellow-agitators.

The inward peace which he so often and so happily calls stillness was not only his finest achievement; it was also the characteristic and shaping element in his style, imparting to his Journal a literary quality of the purest kind. Of this quality he seems to have been entirely unconscious; like many other men of genius, he wrought better than he knew. Expression was, in his intuition, simply a means to an end which was neither artistic nor didactic; but the refinement and harmony of his nature were such that the free and simple utterance of his thought took on the quality of art and was instinct with its charm. There was a touch of Goldsmith's simplicity in him, although nothing of Goldsmith's humor. If to this simplicity are added tranparent sincerity and an easy command of pure English, it is not difficult to understand why Charles Lamb said, "Get the writings of John Woolman by heart"; nor why Henry Crabb Robinson called Woolman "a beautiful soul." "An illiterate tailor, he writes in a style of the most exquisite purity and grace. His moral qualities are transferred to his writings." In the last sentence the charm of Woolman is clearly revealed; his nature was pure and harmonious, and his style, being essentially unconscious, reflected the qualities of his nature. It often happens that men become artists by moral rather than by technical discipline; and being great, bring forth the fruits of greatness in deep and beautiful unconsciousness. "The natural man loveth eloquence," wrote Woolman, "and many love to hear eloquent orations; and if there is not a careful attention to the gift, men who have once labored in the pure Gospel ministry, growing weary of suffering and ashamed of appearing weak, may kindle a fire, compass themselves about with sparks, and walk in the light — not of Christ who is under suffering, but of that fire which they, going from the gift, have kindled; and that, in hearers, which is gone from the meek suffering state into the worldly wisdom, may be warmed with this fire, and speak highly of these labors. That which is of God, gathers to God, and that which is of the world, is owned by the world."

John Woolman was born at Northampton, New Jersey, in the year 1720, in the estate of a farm and in the faith of the Society of Friends. The community, largely made up of Friends, was simple in habit and pervaded by a spirit of thrift and industry. The country was rich in soil and pleasant to the eye. Woolman's Journal barely touches the outward happenings of his youth, being largely a record of the unfolding of his mind and of his spiritual experience. Enough is said, however, to make it clear that he had a growing companionship with nature, and that the quietness of his surroundings in a farming community was favorable to the natural unfolding of a nature which was not only deeply religious but essentially mystical. His educational opportunities must have been slight, although he speaks of himself as "having had schooling pretty well for a planter." More light is thrown upon his training for his work in the sentence, "I used to improve myself in winter evenings, and other leisure times." He was shy and retiring in disposition, finding the company of his own thoughts more enjoyable than that of his fellows; much given to long walks, to meditation, and to sincere searchings of his own heart. "I found it safest for me to live in private, and keep these things sealed up in my own breast." He was meditating on the nature of the religious life, and he was coming to a large and noble view of the relation between God and men. He fastened instinctively upon love as the essential characteristic of divinity, and understood that the worship of such a God must find expression not only in love for Him, but for all His manifestations in the world of nature.

This liberating conception freed him at the start from the intellectual hardness and moral narrowness of many religious people of his time. "I found no narrowness respecting sects and opinions," he writes, "but believed that sincere, upright-hearted people, in every society, who truly love God, were accepted of Him." His creed was simple, inclusive, and fundamental; it was large enough to hold all created things and persons within the circle of divine beneficence, and it was concentrated and effective enough, in its appeal to his own conscience, to make him the self-denying servant of his fellows in slavery.

The Friends in America, like the other colonists, were slaveholders, and no condemnation of the system in any definite way was heard until George Fox, as a result of a visit to Barbadoes in 1671, discussing the essential contradiction between slavery and Christian teaching, began to urge gentleness in dealing with the negro, and gradual emancipation. From this time views of protest against the right of Christians to hold their fellows in bondage began to multiply, and the yearly meetings of the Friends began to debate the question with great earnestness. There was much opposition in many sections to the agitations, for the Friends were thrifty and prosperous and the property interests involved were of great value. In 1742 John Woolman was employed in a small store in the country in which he was born. He was asked by his employer to make a bill of sale of a negro woman; he found the task intensely repugnant to his moral sense, and although he performed it, he frankly declared that he abhorred it, and that he believed the holding and selling of slaves inconsistent with the Christian faith and practice. This was the beginning of his ardent advocacy of emancipations, of which his Journal contains a full and deeply interesting record. Never was a reformer possessed of a deeper love for his fellows or of a more irenic temper than this quiet Friend, who gave his life, without stint or reward, to the work of awakening the consciences of his people until his death in the City of York, England, in the year 1772.

The writing of the Journal was begun when Woolman was thirty-six years old and was continued until his death at the age of fifty-two. He wrote, in the meantime, a number of essays on religious or ethical subjects. The titles — "Considerations on Pure Wisdom and Human Policy, on Labor, on Schools, and on the Right Use of the Lord's Outward Gifts," "Considerations on the True Harmony of Mankind, and how it is to be Maintained," "A Word of Remembrance and Caution to the Rich," and "Some Considerations on the Keeping of Negroes" — show the steady current of Woolman's interests and convictions. He was filled with the passion for humanity, and his works were in harmony with his faith. The labor question, then in the distant future, appealed to him as deeply as the slavery question. "When house is joined to house," he wrote, "and field laid to field, until there is no place, and the poor are thereby straitened, though this done by bargain and purchase, yet so far as it stands distinguished from universal love, so far that woe predicted by the prophet will accompany their proceedings."

The Journal is not a great piece of literature, but it has a quality which separates it from nearly all the writing which preceded or immediately followed it in the colonies. With Jonathan Edwards and Benjamin Franklin, John Woolman must be counted as possessing the literary gift in colonial times, and making a contribution of enduring interest, not only to one literary history, but to our literature. It is interesting to note that the two pieces of writing which may be classed as literature which have come down from pre-Revolutionary day are autobiographies; but beyond similarity of form the Autobiography of Franklin and the Journal of Woolman have almost nothing in common.

THE TESTIMONY OF FRIENDS

In Yorkshire, at their Quarterly Meeting held at York, the 24th and 25th of the third month, 1773, *concerning* JOHN WOOLMAN, *of Mount Holly, in the province of New Jersey, in America, who departed this life at the house of our friend Thomas Priestman, in the suburbs of this city, the 7th of the tenth month,* 1772, *and was interred in the burying-ground of Friends, the 9th of the same, aged about fifty-two years.*

THIS our valuable friend having been under a religious engagement for some time to visit Friends in this nation, and more especially us in the northern parts, undertook the same with the full concurrence and near sympathy of his friends and brethren at home, as appeared by certificates from the Monthly and Quarterly Meetings to which he belonged, and from the Spring-meeting of Ministers and elders, held at Philadelphia, for Pennsylvania and New Jersey.

He arrived in the city of London at the beginning of the last Yearly Meeting, and after attending that meeting travelled northward, visiting the Quarterly Meetings of Hertfordshire, Buckinghamshire, Northamptonshire, Oxfordshire, and Worcestershire, and divers particular meetings in his way.

He visited many meetings on the west side of this county, also some in Lancashire and Westmoreland, from whence he came to our Quarterly Meeting in the last ninth month; and, though much out of health, yet was enabled to attend all the sittings of that meeting except the last.

His disorder, which proved to be the smallpox, increased speedily upon him, and was very afflicting; under which he was supported in much meekness, patience, and Christian fortitude. To those who attended him in his illness, his mind appeared to be centred in Divine love; under the precious influence whereof we believe he finished his course, and entered into the mansions of everlasting rest.

In the early part of his illness he requested a Friend to write, and then broke forth thus: —

"O Lord my God! the amazing horrors of darkness were gathered around me and covered me all over, and I saw no way to go forth. I felt the misery of my fellow-creatures separated from the Divine harmony, and it was heavier than I could bear — I was crushed down under it. I lifted up my hand, and stretched out my arm, but there was none to help me. I looked round about, and was amazed. In the depths of misery, O Lord! I remembered that thou art omnipotent, that I had called thee Father. I felt that I loved thee, and I was made quiet in thy will. I waited for deliverance from thee, and thou hadst pity upon me, when no man could help me. I saw that meekness under suffering was showed to us in the most affecting example of thy son, and that thou wast teaching me to follow him; and I said, thy will, O Father, be done."

Many more of his weighty expressions might have been inserted here, but it was deemed unnecessary, they being already published.

He was a man endued with a large natural capacity; and being obedient to the manifestations of Divine grace, having in patience and humility endured many deep baptisms, he became thereby sanctified and fitted for the Lord's work, and was truly serviceable in his church. Dwelling in awful fear and watchfulness, he was careful in his public appearances to feel the putting forth of the Divine Hand; so that the spring of the Gospel ministry often flowed through him with great sweetness and purity, as a refreshing stream to the weary travellers towards the city of God. Skilful in dividing the word, he was furnished by Him in whom are hid all the treasures of wisdom and knowledge, to communicate freely to the several states of the people where his lot was cast. His conduct at other times was seasoned with the like watchful circumspection and attention to the guidance of Divine wisdom, which rendered his whole conversation edifying.

He was fully persuaded that, as the life of Christ comes to reign in the earth, all abuse and unnecessary oppression, both of the human and brute creation, will come to an end; but under the sense of a deep revolt, and an overflowing stream of unrighteousness, his life was often a life of mourning.

He was deeply concerned on account of that inhuman and iniquitous practice of making slaves of the people of Africa, or holding them in that state; and on that account we understand he not only wrote some books, but travelled much on the continent of America, in order to make the negro masters, especially those in profession with us, sensible of the evil of such a practice; and though in this journey to England he was far removed from the outward sight of their sufferings, yet his deep exercise of mind remained, as appears by a short treatise he wrote in this journey, and his frequent concern to open the miserable state of this deeply injured people. His testimony in the last meeting he attended was on this subject, wherein he remarked, that as we as a Society, when under outward sufferings, had often found it our concern to lay them before those in authority, and thereby, in the Lord's time, had obtained relief, so he recommended this oppressed part of the creation no our notice, that, as way may open, we may represent their sufferings in an individual, if not a Society, capacity to those in authority.

Deeply sensible that the desire to gratify people's inclinations in luxury and superfluities is the principal ground of oppression, and the occasion of many unnecessary wants, he believed it to be his duty to be a pattern of great self-denial with respect to the things of this life, and earnestly to labor with Friends in the meekness of wisdom, to impress on their minds the great importance of our testimony in these things; recommending them to the guidance of the blessed Truth in this and all other concerns, and cautioning such as are inexperienced therein against contenting themselves with acting up to the standard of others, but to be careful to make the standard of Truth manifested to them the measure of their obedience; for said he, "That purity of life which proceeds from faithfulness in following the Spirit of Truth, that state where our minds are devoted to serve God, and all our wants are bounded by his wisdom, this habitation has often been opened before me as a place of retirement for the children of the light, where they may stand separated from that which disordereth and confuseth the affairs of society, and where we may have a testimony of our innocence in the hearts of those who behold us."

We conclude with fervent desires that we as a people may thus, by our example, promote the Lord's work in the earth; and, our hearts being prepared, may unite in prayer to the great Lord of the harvest, that as, in his infinite wisdom, he hath greatly stripped the church, by removing of late divers faithful ministers, and elders, he may be pleased to send forth many more faithful laborers into his harvest.

Signed in, by order, and on behalf of said meeting.

THOMAS BENNETT,	SAMUEL BRISCOE,
JOHN STORR,	JOHN TURNER,
JOSEPH EGLIN,	JOSHUA ROBINSON,
THOMAS PERKINSON,	THOMAS PRIESTMAN,
JOSEPH WRIGHT,	And divers other Friends.

A Testimony of the Monthly Meeting of Friends, held in Burlington, the 1st day of the eighth month, in the year of our Lord, 1774, concerning our esteemed friend JOHN WOOLMAN, *deceased.*

HE was born in Northampton, in the county of Burlington, and province of West New Jersey, in the eighth month, 1720, of religious parents, who instructed him very early in the principles of the Christian religion, as professed by the people called Quakers, which he esteemed a blessing to him, even in his young years, tending to preserve him from the infection of wicked children. But through the workings of the enemy, and the levity incident to youth, he frequently deviated from those parental precepts, by which he laid a renewed foundation for repentance, that was finally succeeded by a godly sorrow not to be repented of, and so became acquainted with that sanctifying power which qualifies for true Gospel ministry, into which he was called about the twenty-second year of his age, and by a faithful use of the talents committed to him, he experienced an increase, until he arrived at the state of a father, capable of dividing the word aright to the different states he ministered unto; dispensing milk to babes, and meat to those of riper years. Thus he found the efficacy of that power to arise, which, in his own expressions, "prepares the creature to stand like a trumpet through which the Lord speaks to his people."

He was a loving husband, a tender father, and very humane to every part of the creation under his care.

His concern for the poor and those in affliction was evident by his visits to them; and he frequently relieved them by his assistance and charity. He was for many years deeply exercised on account of the poor enslaved Africans, whose cause, as he sometimes mentioned, lay almost continually upon him, and to obtain liberty to those captives, he labored both in public and private, and was favored to see his endeavors crowned with considerable success. He was particularly desirous that Friends should not be instrumental to lay burthens on this oppressed people, but remember the days of suffering from which they had been providentially delivered, that if times of trouble should return, no injustice dealt to those in slavery might rise in judgment against us, but, being clear, we might on such occasions address the Almighty with a degree of confidence, for his interposition and relief; being particularly careful as to himself, not to countenance slavery, even by the use of those conveniences of life which were furnished by their labor.

He was desirous to have his own mind, and the minds of others, redeemed from the pleasures and immoderate profits of this world, and to fix them on those joys which fade not away; his principal care being after a life of purity, endeavoring to avoid not only the grosser pollutions, but those also, which appearing in a more refined dress, are not sufficiently guarded against by some well-disposed people. In the latter part of his life he was remarkable for the plainness and simplicity of his dress, and as much as possible, avoided the use of plate, costly furniture and feasting; thereby endeavoring to become an example of temperance and self-denial, which he believed himself called unto, and was favored with peace therein, although it carried the appearance of great austerity in the view of some. He was very moderate in his charges in the way of business, and in his desires after gain; and though a man of industry, avoided and strove much to lead others out of extreme labor and anxiousness after perishable things; being desirous that the strength of our bodies might not be spent in procuring things unprofitable, and that we might use moderation and kindness to the brute animals under our care, to prize the use of them as a great favor, and by no means to abuse them; that the gifts of Providence should be thankfully received and applied to the uses they were designed for.

He several times opened a school at Mount Holly, for the instruction of poor Friends' children and others, being concerned for their help and improvement therein. His love and care for the rising youth among us was truly great, recommending to parents and those who have the charge of them, to choose conscientious and pious tutors, saying, "It is a lovely sight to behold innocent children," and "to labor for their help against that which would mar the beauty of their minds, is a debt we owe them."

His ministry was sound, very deep and penetrating, sometimes pointing out the dangerous situation which indulgence and custom lead into; frequently exhorting others, especially the youth, not to be discouraged at the difficulties which occur, but to press after purity. He often expressed an earnest engagement that pure wisdom should be attended to, which would lead into lowliness of mind and resignation to the Divine will, in which state small possessions here would be sufficient.

In transacting the affairs of discipline, his judgment was sound and clear, and he was very useful in treating with those who had done amiss: he visited such in a private way in that plainness which Truth dictates, showing great tenderness and Christian forbearance. He was a constant attender of our Yearly Meeting, in which he was a good example, and particularly useful; assisting in the business thereof with great weight and attention. He several times visited most of the meetings of the Friends in this and the neighboring provinces, with the concurrence of the Monthly Meeting to which he belonged, and we have reason to believe had good service therein, generally or always expressing at his return how it had fared with him, and the evidence of peace in his mind for thus performing his duty. He was often concerned with other

Friends in the important service of visiting families, which he was enabled to go through to satisfaction.

In the minutes of the meeting of ministers and elders for this quarter, at the foot of a list of the members of that meeting, made about five years before his death, we find in his hand-writing the following observation and reflections. "As looking over the minutes made by persons who have put off this body, hath sometimes revived in me a thought how ages pass away; so this list may probably revive a like thought in some, when I and the rest of the persons above-named, are centred in another state of being. — The Lord, who was the guide of my youth, hath in tender mercies helped me hitherto; he hath healed me of wounds, he hath helped me out of grievous entanglements; he remains to be the strength of my life; to whom I desire to devote myself in time and in eternity.

"Signed, JOHN WOOLMAN."

In the twelfth month, 1771, he acquainted this meeting that he had found his mind drawn towards a religious visit to Friends in some parts of England, particularly in Yorkshire. In the first month, 1772, he obtained our certificate, which was approved and endorsed by our Quarterly Meeting, and by the Half-year's meeting of ministers and elders at Philadelphia. He embarked on his voyage in the fifth, and arrived in London in the sixth month following, at the time of their annual meeting in that city. During his short visit to Friends in that kingdom, we are informed that his services were acceptable and edifying. In his last illness he uttered many lively and comfortable expressions, being "perfectly resigned, having no will either to live or die," as appears by the testimony of Friends at York, in Great Britain, in the suburbs whereof, at the house of our friend Thomas Priestman, he died of the smallpox, on the 7th day of the tenth month, 1772, and was buried in Friends' burying-ground in that city, on the 9th of the same, after a large and solid meeting held on the occasion, aged nearly fifty-two years; a minister upwards of thirty years, during which time he belonged to Mount Holly particular meeting, which he diligently attended when at home and in health of body, and his labors of love and pious care for the prosperity of Friends in the blessed Truth, we hope may not be forgotten, but that his good works may be remembered to edification.

Signed in, and by order of the said meeting, by

SAMUEL ALLINSON, Clerk.

Read and approved at our Quarterly Meeting, held at Burlington the 29th of the eighth month, 1774.

Signed by order of said meeting,

DANIEL SMITH, Clerk.

LIFE OF JOHN WOOLMAN

CHAPTER I

His birth and parentage with some account of the operations of Divine grace on his mind in his youth — His first appearance in the ministry — Considerations while young on keeping slaves.

I HAVE often felt a motion of love to leave some hints in writing of my experience of the goodness of God; and now, in the thirty-sixth year of my, ageI begin this work.

I was born in Northampton, in Burlington county, West Jersey, in the year 1720; and before I was seven years old I began to be acquainted with the operations of Divine love. Through the care of my parents, I was taught to read nearly as soon as I was capable of it; and as I went from school one seventh-day, I remember, while my companions went to play by the way, I went forward out of sight, and sitting down, I read the twenty-second chapter of the Revelation: "He showed me a pure river of water of life, clear as crystal, proceeding out of the throne of God and of the lamb," etc.; and in reading it, my mind was drawn to seek after that pure habitation, which, I then believed, God had prepared for his servants. The place where I sat, and the sweetness that attended my mind, remain fresh in my memory.

This, and the like gracious visitations, had such an effect upon me, that when boys used ill language, it troubled me; and through the continued mercies of God, I was preserved from it.

The pious instructions of my parents were often fresh in my mind when I happened to be among wicked children, and were of use to me. My parents having a large family of children, used frequently, on first days, after meeting, to put us to read in the Holy Scriptures, or some religious books, one after another, the rest sitting by without much conversation; which I have since often thought was a good practice. From what I had read and heard, I believed there had been, in past ages, people who walked in uprightness before God, in a degree exceeding any that I knew or heard of, now living; and the apprehension of there being less steadiness and firmness amongst people in this age than in past ages, often troubled me while I was a child.

A thing remarkable in my childhood was, that once, going to a neighbor's house, I saw, on the way, a robin sitting on her nest; and as I came near she went off, but, having young ones, flew about, and with many cries expressed her concern for them. I stood and threw stones at her, till one striking her, she fell down dead. At first I was pleased with the exploit; but after a few minutes was seized with horror, for having, in a sportive way, killed an innocent creature while she was careful for her young. I beheld her lying dead, and thought those young ones, for which she was so careful, must now perish for want of their dam to nourish them; and after some painful considerations on the subject, I climbed up the tree, took all the young birds, and killed them — supposing that better than to leave them to pine away and die miserably; and believed, in this case, that Scripture proverb was fulfilled, "The tender mercies of the wicked are cruel." I then went on my errand, but, for some hours, could think of little else but the cruelties I had committed, and was much troubled. Thus He, whose tender mercies are over all his works, hath placed a principle in the human mind, which incites to exercise goodness towards every living creature; and this being singly attended to, people become tender-hearted and sympathizing; but being frequently and totally rejected, the mind becomes shut up in a contrary disposition.

About the twelfth year of my age, my father being abroad, my mother reproved me for some misconduct, to which I made an undutiful reply; and the next first-day, as I was with my father returning from meeting, he told me he understood I had behaved amiss to my mother, and advised me to be more careful in future. I knew myself blamable, and in shame and confusion remained silent. Being thus awakened to a sense of my wickedness, I felt remorse in my mind, and getting home, I retired and prayed to the Lord to forgive me; and do not remember that I ever, after that, spoke unhandsomely to either of my parents, however foolish in some other things.

Having attained the age of sixteen years, I began to love wanton company; and though I was preserved from profane language, or scandalous conduct, still I perceived a plant in me which produced many wild grapes. Yet my merciful Father forsook me not utterly, but at times, through his grace, I was brought seriously to consider my ways; and the sight of my backslidings affected me with sorrow; but for want of rightly attending to the reproofs of instruction, vanity was added to vanity, and repentance to repentance. Upon the whole, my mind was more and more alienated from the Truth, and I hastened toward destruction.° While I meditate on the gulf towards which I travelled, and reflect on my youthful disobedience, for these things I weep, mine eye runneth down with water.

Advancing in age, the number of my acquaintance increased, and thereby my way grew more difficult. Though I had found comfort in reading the Holy Scriptures, and thinking on heavenly things, I was now estranged therefrom. I knew I was going from the flock of Christ, and had no resolution to return; hence serious reflections were uneasy to me, and youthful vanities and diversions my greatest pleasure. Running in this road I found many like myself; and we associated in that which is the reverse to true friendship.

But in this swift race it pleased God to visit me with sickness, so that I doubted of recovering; and then did darkness, horror, and amazement, with full force seize me, even when my pain and distress of body were very great. I thought it would have been better for me never to have had a being, than to see the day which I now saw. I was filled with confusion; and in great affliction, both of mind and body, I lay and bewailed myself. I had not confidence to lift up my cries to God, whom I had thus offended; but in a deep sense of my great folly, I was humbled before him: and at length, that word which is as a fire and a hammer, broke and dissolved my rebellious heart, and then my cries were put up in contrition; and in the multitude of his mercies I found inward relief, and felt a close engagement, that if he was pleased to restore my health, I might walk humbly before him.

After my recovery, this exercise remained with me a considerable time; but by degrees, giving way to youthful vanities, they gained strength, and getting with wanton young people I lost ground. The Lord had been very gracious, and had spoken peace to me in the time of my distress; and I now most ungratefully turned again to folly; on which account, at times, I felt sharp reproof, but did not get low enough to cry for help. I was not so hardy as to commit things scandalous; but to exceed in vanity and promote mirth, was my chief study. Still I retained a love and esteem for pious people; and their company brought an awe upon me. My dear parents several times admonished me in the fear of the Lord, and their admonition entered into my heart, and had a good effect for a season; but not getting deep enough to pray rightly, the tempter, when he came, found entrance. I remember that once, having spent a part of the day in wantonness, as I went to bed at night, there lay in a window near my bed a Bible, which I opened, and first cast my eye on the text, "we lie down in our shame, and our confusion covers us"; this I knew to be my case; and meeting with so unexpected a reproof, I was somewhat affected with it, and went to bed under remorse of conscience; which I soon cast off again.

Thus time passed on: my heart was replenished with mirth and wantonness, while pleasing scenes of vanity were presented to my imagination, till I attained the age of eighteen years; near which time I felt the judgments of God in my soul, like a consuming fire; and looking over my past life, the prospect was moving. I was often sad, and longed to be delivered from those vanities; then, again, my heart was strongly inclined to them, and there was in me a sore conflict. At times I turned to folly; and then again, sorrow and confusion took hold of me. In a while, I resolved totally to leave off some of my vanities; but there was a secret reserve in my heart, of the more refined part of them, and I was not low enough to find true peace. Thus for some months, I had great troubles, there remaining in me an unsubjected will, which rendered my labors fruitless, till at length, through the merciful continuance of heavenly visitations, I was made to bow down in spirit before the Lord. I remember one evening I had spent some time in reading a pious author; and walking out alone, I humbly prayed to the Lord for his help, that I might be delivered from all those vanities which so ensnared me. Thus, being brought low, he helped me; and as I learned to bear the cross, I felt refreshment to come from his presence; but not keeping in that strength which gave victory, I lost ground again; the sense of which greatly affected me; and I sought deserts and lonely places, and there with tears did confess my sins to God, and humbly craved help of him. I may say with reverence, he was near to me in my troubles, and in those times of humiliation opened my ear to discipline. I was now led to look seriously at the means by which I was drawn from the pure truth, and learned this, that if I would live in the life which the faithful servants of God lived in, I must not go into company as heretofore, in my own will; but all the cravings of sense must be governed by a Divine principle. In times of sorrow and abasement, these instructions were sealed upon me, and I felt the power of Christ prevail over selfish desires, so that I was preserved in a good degree of steadiness; and being young, and believing, at that time, that a single life was best for me, I was strengthened to keep from such company as had often been a snare to me.

I kept steadily to meetings; spent first-day° afternoon chiefly in reading the Scriptures, and other good books; and was early convinced in my mind that true religion consisted in an inward life wherein the heart doth love and reverence God the Creator, and learns to exercise true justice and goodness, not only toward all men, but also toward the brute creatures. That as the mind is moved by an inward principle to love God as an invisible, incomprehensible Being, by the same principle it is moved to love him in all his manifestations in the visible world. That, as by his breath the flame of life was kindled in all sensible creatures, to say we love God as unseen, and, at the same time, exercise cruelty toward the least creature, moving by his life, or by life derived from him, is a contradiction in itself.

I found no narrowness respecting sects and opinions; but believed that sincere, upright-hearted people, in every society, who truly love God, were accepted of him.

As I lived under the cross, and simply followed the openings of Truth, my mind, from day to day, was more enlightened; my former acquaintance were left to judge of me as they would, for I found it safest for me to live in private, and to keep these things sealed up in my own breast. While I silently ponder on that change wrought in me, I find no language equal to [describe] it, nor any means to convey to another a clear idea of it. I looked upon the works of God in this visible creation, and an awfulness covered me; my heart was tender, and often contrite, and universal love to my fellow-creatures increased in me: this will be understood by such who have trodden in the same path.

Some glances of real beauty may be seen in their faces who dwell in true meekness. There is a harmony in the sound of that voice to which Divine love gives utterance, and some appearance of right order in their temper and conduct, whose passions are regulated; yet all these do not fully show forth that inward life to such who have not felt it; but this white stone and new name are known rightly to such only who have them.

Though I had been thus strengthened to bear the cross, I still found myself in great danger, having many weaknesses attending me, and strong temptations to wrestle with; in the feeling whereof I frequently withdrew into private places, and often with tears besought the Lord to help me, whose gracious ear was open to my cry.

All this time I lived with my parents, and wrought on the plantation°; and having had schooling pretty well for a planter, I used to improve it in winter evenings, and other leisure times; and being now in the twenty-first year of my age, a man in much business at shop-keeping and baking asked me if I would hire with him to tend shop and keep books. I acquainted my father with the proposal; and, after some deliberation, it was agreed for me to go.

At home I had lived retired; and now, having a prospect of being much in the way of company, I felt frequent and fervent cries in my heart to God, the Father of mercies, that he would preserve me from all taint and corruption; that, in this more public employment, I might serve Him, my gracious Redeemer, in that humility and self-denial with which I had been, in a small degree, exercised in a more private life. The man who employed me furnished a shop in Mount Holly, about five miles from my father's house, and six from his own ; and there I lived alone, and tended his shop. Shortly after my settlement here, I was visited by several young people, my former acquaintance, who knew not but vanities would be as agreeable to me now as ever ; and at these times I cried to the Lord in secret for wisdom and strength ; for I felt myself encompassed with difficulties, and had fresh occasion to bewail the follies of time past in contracting a familiarity with libertine people ; and as I had now left my father's house outwardly, I found my heavenly Father to be merciful to me beyond what I can express.

By day I was much amongst people, and had many trials to go through ; but in the evenings I was mostly alone, and may with thankfulness acknowledge that, in those times, the spirit of supplication was often poured upon me ; under which I was frequently exercised, and felt my strength renewed.

In a few months after I came here, my master bought several Scotchmen as servants,° from on board a vessel, and brought them to Mount Holly to sell ; one of them was taken sick, and died.

In the latter part of his sickness, he, being delirious, used to curse and swear most sorrowfully ; and the next night after his burial, I was left to sleep alone in the same chamber where he died. I perceived in me a timorousness. I knew, however, that I had not injured the man, but assisted in taking care of him according to my capacity, and was not free to ask any one, on that occasion, to sleep with me. Nature was feeble, but every trial was a fresh incitement to give myself up wholly to the service of God ; for I found no helper like him in times of trouble.

After a while, my former acquaintance gave over expecting me as one of their company ; and I began to be known to some whose conversation was helpful to me. As I had experienced the love of God, through Jesus Christ, to redeem me from many polutions, and to be a succor to me through a sea of conflicts, with which no person was fully acquainted, and as my heart was often enlarged in this heavenly principle, I felt a tender compassion for the youth who remained entangled in snares like those which had entangled me from one time to another. This love and tenderness increased, and my mind was more strongly engaged for the good of my fellow-creatures. I went to meetings in an awful frame of mind, and endeavored to be inwardly acquainted with the language of the true Shepherd; and one day, being under a strong exercise of spirit, I stood up, and said some words in a meeting; but not keeping close to the Divine opening, I said more than was required of me; and being soon sensible of my error, I was afflicted in mind some weeks, without any light or comfort, even to such a degree that I could not take satisfaction in anything. I remembered God, and was troubled; and, in the depth of my distress, he had pity upon me, and sent the Comforter. I then felt forgiveness for my offence, and my mind became calm and quiet, being truly thankful to my gracious Redeemer for his mercies; and after this, feeling the spring of Divine love opened, and a concern to speak, I said a few words in a meeting, in which I found peace. This, I believe, was about six weeks from the first time. As I was thus humbled and disciplined under the cross, my understanding became more strengthened to distinguish the pure spirit which inwardly moves upon the heart, and taught me to wait in silence, sometimes many weeks together, until I felt that rise which prepares the creature to stand like a trumpet, through which the Lord speaks to his flock.

From an inward purifying, and steadfast abiding under it, springs a lively operative desire for the good of others: all the faithful are not called to the public ministry; but whoever are, are called to minister of that which they have tasted and handled spiritually. The outward modes of worship are various; but wherever any are true ministers of Jesus Christ, it is from the operation of his Spirit upon their hearts, first purifying them, and thus giving them a just sense of the condition of others.

This truth was early fixed in my mind; and I was taught to watch the pure opening, and to take heed, lest, while I was standing to speak, my own will should get uppermost, and cause me to utter words from worldly wisdom, and depart from the channel of the true Gospel ministry. In the management of my outward affairs, I may say with thankfulness, I found truth to be my support; and I was respected in my master's family, who came to live in Mount Holly within two years after my going there.

About the twenty-third year of my age, I had many fresh and heavenly openings, in respect to the care and providence of the Almighty over his creatures in general, and over man as the most noble amongst those which are visible. And being clearly convinced in my judgment, that to place my whole trust in God was best for me, I felt renewed engagements that in all things I might act on an inward principle of virtue, and pursue worldly business no further than Truth opened my way therein.

About the time called Christmas,° I observed that many people from the country, and dwellers in town, resorting to public houses, spent their time in drinking and vain sports, tending to corrupt one another; on which account I was much troubled. At one house in particular there was much disorder; and I believed it was a duty incumbent on me to go and speak to the master of that house. I considered I was young, and that several elderly Friends in town had an opportunity to see these things; but though I would gladly have been excused, yet I could not feel my mind clear.

The exercise was heavy; and as I was reading what the Almighty said to Ezekiel, respecting his duty as a watchman, the matter was set home more clearly; and then, with prayers and tears, I besought the Lord for his assistance, who, in loving kindness, gave me a resigned heart. Then, at a suitable opportunity, I went to the public house; and seeing the man amongst much company, I went to him, and told him I wanted to speak with him. So we went aside, and there, in the fear and dread of the Almighty, I expressed to him what rested on my mind; which he took kindly, and afterwards showed more regard to me than before. In a few years afterwards he died, middle-aged; and I often thought, that had I neglected my duty in that case, it would have given me great trouble; and I was humbly thankful to my gracious Father, who had supported me herein.

My employer, having a negro woman,° sold her, and desired me to write a bill of sale, the man being waiting who bought her. The thing was sudden; and though the thoughts of writing an instrument of slavery for one of my fellow-creatures felt uneasy, yet I remembered that I was hired by the year, that it was my master who directed me to do it, and that it was an elderly man, a member of our Society, who bought her, so, through weakness, I gave way, and wrote it; but, at the executing of it, I was so afflicted in my mind that I said, before my master and the Friend, that I believed slave-keeping to be a practice inconsistent with the Christian religion. This in some degree abated my uneasiness; yet, as often as I reflected seriously upon it, I thought I should have been clearer if I had desired to be excused from it, as a thing against my conscience; for such it was. Some time after this, a young man of our Society spoke to me to write a conveyance of a slave to him; he having lately taken a negro into his house. I told him I was not easy to write it; for, though many of our meeting and in other places kept slaves, I still believed the practice was not right, and desired to be excused from the writing. I spoke to him in good will, and he told me that keeping slaves was not altogether agreeable to his mind; but that the slave being a gift made to his wife, he had accepted of her.

CHAPTER II

His first journey, on a religious visit, into East Jersey, in company with Abraham Farrington — Thoughts on merchandizing, and learning a trade — Second journey, with Isaac Andrews, into Pennsylvania, Maryland, Virginia, and North Carolina — Third journey, with Peter Andrews, through part of West and East Jersey — Some account of his sister Elizabeth, and her death — Fourth journey, with Peter Andrews, through New York and Long Island, to New England — Fifth journey, with John Sykes, to the Eastern Shore of Maryland, and the lower countries on Delaware.

My esteemed friend, Abraham Farrington, being about to make a visit to Friends° on the eastern side of this province, and having no companion, proposed to me to go with him; and after a conference with some elderly Friends, I agreed to go. We set out on the 5th day of the ninth month,° in the year 1743, and had an evening meeting at a tavern in Brunswick, a town in which none of our Society dwelt; the room was full, and the people quiet. Thence to Amboy, and had an evening meeting in the court-house; to which came many people, amongst whom were several members of Assembly, they being in town on the public affairs of the province: in both these meetings my ancient companion was enlarged to preach in the love of the Gospel. Thence we went to Woodbridge, Rahway, and Plainfield; and had six or seven meetings in places where Friends' meetings are not usually held, being made up chiefly of Presbyterians, and my beloved companion was frequently strengthened to publish the word of life amongst them. As for me, I was often silent through the meetings; and when I spake, it was with much care, that I might speak only what Truth opened: my mind was often tender, and I learned some profitable lessons. We were out about two weeks.

Near this time, being on some outward business in which several families were concerned, and which was attended with difficulties, some things relating thereto not being clearly stated, nor rightly understood by all, there arose some heat in the minds of the parties, and one valuable Friend got off his watch. I had a great regard for him, and felt a strong inclination, after matters were settled, to speak to him concerning his conduct in that case; but I being a youth, and he far advanced in age and experience, my way appeared difficult. But after some days' deliberation, and inward seeking to the Lord for assistance, I was made subject; so that I expressed what lay upon me, in a way which became my youth and his years: and though it was a hard task to me, it was well taken, and, I believe, was useful to us both.

Having now been several years with my employer, and he doing less at merchandise than heretofore, I was thoughtful of some other way of business; perceiving merchandise to be attended with much cumber, in the way of trading in these parts.

My mind, through the power of Truth, was in a good degree weaned from the desire of outward greatness, and I was learning to be content with real conveniences, that were not costly; so that a way of life free from much entanglement, appeared best for me, though the income might be small. I had several offers of business that appeared profitable, but did not see my way clear to accept of them; believing the business proposed would be attended with more outward care and cumber than it was required of me to engage in.

I saw that a humble man, with the blessing of the Lord, might live on a little: and that where the heart was set on greatness, success in business did not satisfy the craving; but that commonly with an increase of wealth, the desire of wealth increased. There was a care on my mind so to pass my time, that nothing might hinder me from the most steady attention to the voice of the true Shepherd.

My employer, though now a retailer of goods, was by trade a tailor, and kept a servant man at that business; and I began to think about learning the trade, expecting, that if I should settle, I might, by this trade, and a little retailing of goods, get a living in a plain way, without the load of great business. I mentioned it to my employer, and we soon agreed on terms; and then, when I had leisure from the affairs of merchandize, I worked with this man. I believed the hand of Providence pointed out this business for me; and was taught to be content with it, though I felt, at times, a disposition that would have sought for something greater. But, through the revelation of Jesus Christ, I had seen the happiness of humility, and there was an earnest desire in me to enter deeply into it; and, at times, this desire arose to a degree of fervent supplication, wherein my soul was so environed with heavenly light and consolation, that things were made easy to me which had been otherwise.

After some time, my employer's wife died; she was a virtuous woman, and generally beloved of her neighbors: and soon after this, he left shop-keeping; and we parted. I then wrought at my trade, as a tailor; carefully attended meetings for worship and discipline; and found an enlargement of Gospel love in my mind, and therein a concern to visit Friends in some of the back settlements of Pennsylvania and Virginia. Being thoughtful about a companion, I expressed it to my beloved friend Isaac Andrews, who then told me that he had drawings to the same places; and also to go through Maryland, Virginia, and Carolina. After considerable time passed, and several conferences with him, I felt easy to accompany him throughout, if way opened for it. I opened the case in our Monthly Meeting, and friends expressing their unity therewith, we obtained certificates to travel as companions; his from Haddonfield, and mine from Burlington.

We left our province on the 12th day of the third month, in the year 1746, and had several meetings in the upper part of Chester county near Lancaster; in some of which, the love of Christ prevailed, uniting us together in his service. Then we crossed the river Susquehanna, and had several meetings in a new settlement, called the Red-lands; the oldest of which, as I was informed, did not exceed ten years. It is the poorer sort of people who commonly begin to improve remote deserts: with a small stock they have houses to build, lands to clear and fence, corn to raise, clothes to provide, and children to educate; that Friends, who visit such, may well sympathize with them in their hardships in the wilderness; and though the best entertainment such can give, may seem coarse to some who are used to cities, or old-settled places, it becomes the disciples of Christ to be content with it. Our hearts were sometimes enlarged in the love of our heavenly Father amongst these people; and the sweet influence of his Spirit supported us through some difficulties: to him be the praise.

We passed on to Manoquacy, Fairfax, Hopewell, and Shanandoah, and had meetings; some of which were comfortable and edifying. From Shanandoah we set off in the afternoon for the old settlements of Friends in Virginia; and the first night, we, with our pilot, lodged in the woods, our horses feeding near us; but he being poorly provided with a horse, and we young and having good horses, were free to part with him; and next day did so. In two days after, we reached our friend John Cheagle's, in Virginia; and taking the meetings in our way through Virginia, were, in some degree, baptized into a feeling of the conditions of the people; and our exercise in general was more painful in these old settlements, than it had been amongst the back inhabitants: but through the goodness of our heavenly Father, the well of living waters was, at times, opened to our encouragement and the refreshment of the sincere-hearted. We went on to Perquimons, in North Carolina; had several meetings, which were large, and found some openness in those parts, and a hopeful appearance among the young people. We turned again into Virginia, and attended most of the meetings which we had not been at before, laboring amongst Friends in the love of Jesus Christ, as ability was given; and thence went to the mountains, up James River to a settlement, and had several meetings amongst the people, some of whom had lately joined in membership with our Society. In our journeying to and fro, we found some honest-hearted Friends, who appeared to be concerned for the cause of Truth, among a backsliding people.

From Virginia, we crossed over the river Potomac, at Hoe's ferry, and made a general visit to the meetings of Friends on the Western Shore of Maryland, and were at their Quarterly Meeting.° We had some hard labor amongst them, endeavoring to discharge our duty honestly as way opened, in the love of truth. Taking sundry meetings in our way, we passed homeward, where, through the favor of Divine Providence, we reached, the 16th day of the sixth month, in the year 1746; and I may say, that through the assistance of the Holy Spirit, which mortifies selfish desires, my companion and I travelled in harmony, and parted in the nearness of true brotherly love.

Two things were remarkable to me in this journey: first, in regard to my entertainment; when I eat, drank, and lodged free-cost, with people who lived in ease on the hard labor of their slaves, I felt uneasy; and as my mind was inward to the Lord, I found, from place to place, this uneasiness return upon me, at times, through the whole visit. Where the masters bore a good share of the burthen, and lived frugally, so that their servants were well provided for, and their labor moderate, I felt more easy; but where they lived in a costly way, and laid heavy burthens on their slaves, my exercise was often great, and I frequently had conversation with them, in private, concerning it. Secondly; the trade of importing slaves from their native country being much encouraged amongst them, and the white people and their children so generally living without much labor, were frequently the subjects of my serious thoughts; and I saw in these southern provinces so many vices and corruptions, increased by this trade and this way of life, that it appeared to me as a dark gloominess hanging over the land; and though now many willingly run into it, yet in future the consequences will be grievous to posterity. I express it as it hath appeared to me, not at once, or twice, but as a matter fixed on my mind.

Soon after my return home, I felt an increasing concern for Friends on our sea-coast; and on the 8th day of the eighth month, in the year 1746, with the unity of Friends, and in company with my beloved friend and neighbor Peter Andrews, brother to my companion before mentioned, I set forward, and visited meetings generally about Salem, Cape May, Great and Little Egg Harbor, and had meetings at Barnagat, Mannahockin, and Mane-Squan, and so to the Yearly Meeting at Shrewsbury. Through the goodness of the Lord, way was opened, and the strength of Divine love was sometimes felt in our assemblies, to the comfort and help of those who were rightly concerned before him. We were out twenty-two days, and rode, by computation, three hundred and forty miles. At Shrewsbury Yearly Meeting, we met with our dear friends Michael Lightfoot and Abraham Farrington, who had good service there.

The winter following died my eldest sister, Elizabeth Woolman, Jun., of the smallpox, aged thirty-one years. She was, from her youth, of a thoughtful disposition, and very compassionate to her acquaintances in their sickness or distress, being ready to help as far as she could. She was dutiful to her parents; one instance whereof follows: It happened that she and two of her sisters, being then near the estate of young women, had an inclination one first-day, after meeting, to go on a visit to some other young women, at some distance off, whose company I believe would have done them no good. They expressed their desire to our parents; who were dissatisfied with the proposal, and stopped them. The same day, as my sisters and I were together, and they talking about their disappointment, Elizabeth expressed her contentment under it; signifying she believed it might be for their good.

A few years after she attained to mature age, through the gracious visitations of God's love, she was strengthened to live a self-denying, exemplary life, giving herself much to reading and meditation.

The following letter may show, in some degree, her disposition: —

HADDONFIELD, Eleventh Month, 1st, 1743.

BELOVED BROTHER, JOHN WOOLMAN: — In that love which desires the welfare of all men, I write unto thee. I received thine, dated 2d day of the tenth month last, with which I was comforted. My spirit was bowed with thankfulness that I should be remembered, who am unworthy; but the Lord is full of mercy, and his goodness is extended to the meanest of his creation; therefore, in his infinite love, he hath pitied, and spared, and showed mercy, that I have not been cut off nor quite lost; but at times I am refreshed and comforted as with the glimpse of his presence, which is more to the immortal part than all which this world can afford: so, with desires for thy preservation with my own, I remain

Thy affectionate sister,

ELIZABETH WOOLMAN, JUN.

The fore part of her illness she was in great sadness and dejection of mind, of which she told one of her intimate friends, and said, When I was a young girl I was wanton and airy, but I thought I had thoroughly repented for it; and added, I have of late had great satisfaction in meetings. Though she was thus disconsolate, still she retained a hope, which was as an anchor to her: and some time after, the same friend came again to see her, to whom she mentioned her former expressions, and said, It is otherwise now; for the Lord hath rewarded me sevenfold, and I am unable to express the greatness of his love manifested to me. Her disorder appearing dangerous, and our mother being sorrowful, she took notice of it, and said, Dear mother, weep not for me; I go to my God: and many times, with an audible voice, uttered praise to her Redeemer.

A Friend coming some miles to see her the morning before she died, asked her how she did. She answered, I have had a hard night, but shall not have another such; for I shall die, and it will be well with my soul. And accordingly she died the next evening.

The following ejaculations were found amongst her writings; written, I believe, at four times: —

I. Oh that my head were as waters, and mine eyes as a fountain of tears! that I might weep day and night, until acquainted with my God.

II. O Lord, that I may enjoy thy presence! or else my time is lost, and my life a snare to my soul.

III. O Lord, that I may receive bread from thy table, and that thy grace may abound in me!

IV. O Lord, that I may be acquainted with thy presence, that I may be seasoned with salt, that thy grace may abound in me!

Of late I found drawings in my mind to visit Friends in New England; and having an opportunity of joining in company with my beloved friend Peter Andrews, we having obtained certificates from our Monthly Meeting, and set forward on the 16th day of the third month, in the year 1747, and reached the yearly meeting° at Long Island; at which were our friends Samuel Nottingham, from England, John Griffith, Jane Hoskins, and Elizabeth Hudson, from Pennsylvania, and Jacob Andrews, from Chesterfield; several of whom were favored in their public exercise; and, through the goodness of the Lord, we had some edifying meetings. After this, my companion and I visited Friends on Long Island; and, through the mercies of God, we were helped in the work.

Besides going to the settled meetings of Friends, we were at a general meeting at Setawket, chiefly made up of other societies, and had a meeting at Oyster Bay, in a dwelling-house, at which were many people: at the first of which there was not much said by way of testimony; but it was, I believe, a good meeting: at the latter, through the springing up of living waters, it was a day to be thankfully remembered. Having visited the island, we went over to the main, taking meetings in our way to Oblong, Nine-Partners, and New Milford. In these back settlements we met with several people, who, through the immediate workings of the Spirit of Christ on their minds, were drawn from the vanities of the world to an inward acquaintance with him: they were educated in the way of the Presbyterians. A considerable number of the youth, members of that Society, were used to spend their time often together in merriment; but some of the principal young men of that company being visited by the powerful workings of the Spirit of Christ, and thereby led humbly to take up his cross, could no longer join in those vanities; and as these stood steadfast to that inward convincement, they were made a blessing to some of their former companions; so that, through the power of Truth, several were brought into a close exercise concerning the eternal well-being of their souls. These young people continued for a time to frequent their public worship; and besides that, had meetings of their own; which meetings were a while allowed by their preacher, who sometimes met with them: but, in time, their judgment in matters of religion disagreeing with some of the articles of the Presbyterians, their meetings were disapproved by that Society; and such of them who stood firm to their duty, as it was inwardly manifested, had many difficulties to go through. Their meetings were, in a while, dropped; some of them returning to the Presbyterians, and others, after a time, joined our religious Society.

I had conversation with some of the latter, to my help and edification; and believe several of them are acquainted with the nature of that worship which is performed in spirit and in truth. From hence, accompanied by Amos Powel, a Friend from Long Island, we rode through Connecticut, chiefly inhabited by Presbyterians; who were generally civil to us, so far as I saw: and after three days' riding, we came amongst Friends in the colony of Rhode Island. We visited Friends in and about Newport and Dartmouth, and generally in those parts, and then went to Boston, and proceeded eastward as far as Dover; then returned to Newport, and not far from thence we met our friend, Thomas Gawthrop, from England, who was then on a visit to these provinces. From Newport we sailed to Nantucket; were there nearly a week, and from thence came over to Dartmouth: and having finished our visits in these parts, we crossed the sound from New London to Long Island; and taking some meetings on the island, proceeded homeward; where we reached the 13th day of the seventh month, in the year 1747, having rode about fifteen hundred miles, and sailed about one hundred and fifty.

In this journey, I may say in general, we were sometimes in much weakness, and labored under discouragements; and at other times, through the renewed manifestations of Divine love, we had seasons of refreshment, wherein the power of Truth prevailed.

We were taught, by renewed experience, to labor for an inward stillness; at no time to seek for words, but to live in the Spirit of Truth, and utter that to the people which Truth opened in us. My beloved companion and I belonged to one meeting, came forth in the ministry near the same time, and were inwardly united in the work: he was about thirteen years older than I, bore the heaviest burthen, and was an instrument of the greatest use.

Finding a concern to visit friends in the lower counties on Delaware, and on the Eastern Shore of Maryland, and having an opportunity to join with my well-beloved ancient friend John Sykes, we obtained certificates, and set off the 7th day of the eighth month, in the year 1748; were at the meeting of Friends in the lower counties, attended the Yearly Meeting at Little Creek, and made a visit to most of the meetings on the Eastern Shore; and so home by the way of Nottingham: were abroad about six weeks, and rode, by computation, about five hundred and fifty miles.

Our exercise, at times, was heavy; but, through the goodness of the Lord, we were often refreshed: and I may say, by experience, "He is a strong hold in the day of trouble." Though our Society, in these parts, appeared to me to be in a declining condition, yet I believe the Lord hath a people amongst them who labor to serve him uprightly, but have many difficulties to encounter.

CHAPTER III

His marriage — The death of his father — His journeys into the upper part of New Jersey, and afterwards into Pennsylvania — Considerations on keeping slaves — Visits to the families of Friends at several times and places — An epistle from the General Meeting — Journey to Long Island — Considerations on trading, and on the use of spirituous liquors and costly apparel — Letter to a Friend.

About this time, believing it good for me to settle, and thinking seriously about a companion, my heart was turned to the Lord, with desires that he would give me wisdom to proceed therein agreeably to his will; and he was pleased to give me a well-inclined damsel, Sarah Ellis; to whom I was married the 18th day of the eighth month, in the year 1749.

In the fall of the year 1850, died my father, Samuel Woolman, with a fever, aged about sixty years.

In his lifetime he manifested much care for us his children, that in our youth we might learn to fear the Lord; often endeavoring to imprint in our minds the true principles of virtue, and particularly to cherish in us a spirit of tenderness, not only towards poor people, but also towards all creatures of which we had the command.

After my return from Carolina, in the year 1746, I made some observations on keeping slaves, which some time before his decease I showed him. He perused the manuscript, proposed a few alterations, and appeared well satisfied that I found a concern on that account. In his last sickness, as I was watching with him one night, he being so far spent that there was no expectation of his recovery, but had the perfect use of his understanding, he asked me concerning the manuscript, whether I expected soon to proceed to take the advice of Friends in publishing it; and, after some conversation thereon, said, I have all along been deeply affected with the oppression of the poor negroes; and now, at last, my concern for them is as great as ever.

By his direction, I had written his will in a time of health, and that night he desired me to read it to him, which I did; and he said it was agreeable to his mind. He then made mention of his end, which he believed was now near, and signified that, though he was sensible of many imperfections in the course of his life, yet his experience of the power of Truth, and of the love and goodness of God from time to time, even until now, was such that he had no doubt but that, in leaving this life, he should enter into one more happy.

The next day his sister Elizabeth came to see him, and told him of the decease of their sister Ann; who died a few days before. He said, I reckon sister Ann was free to leave this world? Elizabeth said she was. He then said, I also am free to leave it; and being in great weakness of body, said, I hope I shall shortly go to rest. He continued in a weighty frame of mind, and was sensible until near the last.

On the 2d day of the ninth month, in the year 1751, feeling drawings in my mind to visit Friends at the Great Meadows, in the upper part of West Jersey, with the unity of our Monthly Meeting, I went there, and had some searching, laborious exercise amongst Friends in those parts, and found inward peace therein.

In the ninth month of the year 1753, in company with my well-esteemed friend John Sykes, and with the unity of Friends, I travelled about two weeks, visiting Friends in Bucks county. We labored in the love of the Gospel, according to the measure received; and, through the mercies of Him who is strength to the poor who trust in Him, we found satisfaction in our visit.

In the next winter, way opening to visit Friends' families within the compass of our Monthly Meeting, partly by the labors of two Friends from Pennsylvania, I joined in some part of the work; having had a desire for some time that it might go forward amongst us.

About this time, a person at some distance lying sick, his brother came to me to write his will. I knew he had slaves; and asking his brother, was told he intended to leave them as slaves to his children. As writing is a profitable employ, and as offending sober people was disagreeable to my inclination, I was straitened in my mind; but as I looked to the Lord, he inclined my heart to his testimony. I told the man that I believed the practice of continuing slavery to this people was not right, and had a scruple in my mind against doing writings of that kind; that, though many in our Society kept them as slaves, still I was not easy to be concerned in it, and desired to be excused from going to write the will. I spake to him in the fear of the Lord; and he made no reply to what I said, but went away: he also had some concern in the practice, and I thought he was displeased with me. In this case, I had a fresh confirmation that acting contrary to present outward interest, from a motive of Divine love, and in regard to truth and righteousness, and thereby incurring the resentments of people, opens the way to a treasure better than silver, and to a friendship exceeding the friendship of men.

The manuscript before mentioned having laid by me several years, the publication of it rested weightily upon me; and this year I offered it to the revisal of Friends, who, having examined and made some small alterations in it, directed a number of copies thereof to be published and dispersed amongst Friends.

In the year 1754, I found my mind drawn to join in a visit to Friends' families belonging to Chesterfield Monthly Meeting; and having the approbation of our own, I went to their Monthly Meeting in order to confer with Friends, and see if way opened for it. I had conference with some of their members, the proposal having been opened before in their meeting, and one Friend agreed to join with me as a companion for a beginning; but when meeting was ended, I felt great distress of mind, and doubted what way to take, or whether to go home and wait for greater clearness. I kept my distress secret; and going with a Friend to his house, my desires were to the great Shepherd for his heavenly instruction; and in the morning I felt easy to proceed on the visit, being very low in my mind: and as mine eye was turned to the Lord, waiting in families in deep reverence before him, he was pleased graciously to afford help; so that we had many comfortable opportunities, and it appeared as a fresh visitation to some young people. I spent several weeks this winter in the service; part of which time was employed near home. In the following winter I was several weeks in the same service; some part of the time at Shrewsbury, in company with my beloved friend John Sykes; and have cause humbly to acknowledge that, through the goodness of the Lord, our hearts were, at times, enlarged in his love, and strength was given to go through the trials which, in the course of our visit, attended us.

From a disagreement between the powers of England and France, it was now a time of trouble on this continent; and an epistle to Friends went forth from our General Spring Meeting, which I thought good to give a place in this journal.

An Epistle from our General Spring Meeting of ministers and elders, for Pennsylvania and New Jersey, held at Philadelphia, from the 29th of the third month to the 1st of the fourth month, inclusive, 1755: To Friends on the continent of America.

DEAR FRIENDS:—In an humble sense of Divine goodness, and the gracious continuation of God's love to his people, we tenderly salute you; and are at this time therein engaged in mind, that all of us who profess the Truth, as held forth and published by our worthy predecessors in this latter age of the world, may keep near to that Life which is the Light of men, and be strengthened to hold fast the profession of our faith without wavering, that our trust may not be in man, but in the Lord alone, who ruleth in the army of heaven, and in the kingdoms of men, before whom the earth is "as the dust of the balance, and her inhabitants as grasshoppers."

We, being convinced that the gracious design of the Almighty in sending his Son into the world was to repair the breach made by disobedience, to finish sin and transgression, that his kingdom might come, and his will be done on earth as it is in heaven, have found it to be our duty to cease from those national contests productive of misery and bloodshed, and submit our cause to Him the Most High, whose tender love to his children exceeds the most warm affections of natural parents, and who hath promised to his seed throughout the earth, as to one individual, "I will never leave thee, nor forsake thee." And as we, through the gracious dealings of the Lord our God, have had experience of that work which is carried on, "not by *earthly* might, nor by power, but by my Spirit, saith the Lord of Hosts"; by which operation, that spiritual kingdom is set up, which is to subdue and break in pieces all kingdoms that oppose it, and shall stand forever; in a deep sense thereof, and of the safety, stability, and peace there is in it, we are desirous that all who profess the Truth may be inwardly acquainted with it, and thereby be qualified to conduct in all parts of our life as becomes our peaceable profession. And we trust, as there is a faithful continuance to depend wholly upon the Almighty arm, from one generation to another, the peaceable kingdom will gradually be extended "from sea to sea, and from the river to the ends of the earth," to the completion of those prophecies already begun, that "nation shall not lift up sword against nation, neither shall they learn war any more."

And, dearly beloved friends, seeing we have these promises, and believe that God is beginning to fulfil them, let us constantly endeavor to have our minds sufficiently disentangled from the surfeiting cares of this life, and redeemed from the love of the world, that no earthly possessions or enjoyments may bias our judgments, or turn us from that resignation and entire trust in God to which his blessing is most surely annexed; then may we say, "Our Redeemer is mighty, he will plead our cause for us." And if, for the further promoting of his most gracious purposes in the earth, he should give us to taste of that bitter cup which his faithful ones have often partaken of, oh that we may be rightly prepared to receive it!

And now, dear friends, with respect to the commotions and stirrings of the powers of the earth at this time near us, we are desirous that none of us may be moved thereat; "but repose ourselves in the munition of that Rock, that all these shakings shall not move, even in the knowledge and feeling of the eternal power of God, keeping us subjectly given up to his heavenly will, and feel it daily to mortify that which remains in any of us which is of this world; for the worldly part in any is the changeable part; and that is up and down, full and empty, joyful and sorrowful, as things go well or ill in this world. For as the Truth is but one, and many are made partakers of its spirit, so the world is but one, and many are made partakers of the spirit of it; and so many as do partake of it will be straitened and perplexed with it. But they who are single to the Truth, waiting daily to feel the life and virtue of it in their hearts, shall rejoice in the midst of adversity," and have to experience with the prophet, that "Although the fig tree shall not blossom, neither shall fruit be in the vines; the labor of the olive shall fail, and the fields shall yield no meat; the flock shall be cut off from the fold, and there shall be no herd in the stalls; yet will they rejoice in the Lord, and joy in the God of their salvation."

If, contrary to this, we profess the Truth, and, not living under the power and influence of it, are producing fruits disagreeable to the purity thereof, and trust to the strength of man to support ourselves therein, our confidence will be vain. For He, who removed the hedge from his vineyard, and gave it to be trodden under foot, by reason of the wild grapes it produced (Isaiah v. 5), remains unchangeable: and if, for the chastisement of wickedness, and the further promoting his own glory, he doth arise, even to shake terribly the earth, who then may oppose him and prosper?

We remain, in the love of the Gospel, your friends and brethren.

Signed by fourteen Friends.

Scrupling to do writings relative to keeping slaves, having been a means of sundry small trials to me, in which I have evidently felt my own will set aside, I think it good to mention a few of them. Tradesmen and retailers of goods, who depend on their business for a living, are naturally inclined to keep the good will of their customers; nor is it a pleasant thing for young men to be under any necessity to question the judgment or honesty of elderly men, and more especially of such who have a fair reputation. Deep-rooted customs, though wrong, are not easily altered; but it is the duty of every one to be firm in that which they certainly know is right for them. A charitable, benevolent man, well acquainted with a negro, may, I believe, under some circumstances, keep him in his family as a servant, on no other motives than the negro's good; but man, as man, knows not what shall be after him, nor hath he any assurance that his children will attain to that perfection in wisdom and goodness necessary rightly to exercise such power. Hence it is clear to me, that I ought not to be the scribe where wills are drawn in which some children are made absolute masters over others during life.

About this time, an ancient man of good esteem in the neighborhood came to my house to get his will written. He had young negroes, and I asked him privately how he purposed to dispose of them. He told me. I then said, I cannot write thy will without breaking my own peace, and respectfully gave him my reasons for it. He signified that he had a choice that I should have written it; but as I could not, consistent with my conscience, he did not desire it: and so he got it written by some other person. A few years after, there being great alterations in his family, he came again to get me to write his will: his negroes were yet young, and his son, to whom he intended to give them, was, since he first spoke to me, from a libertine, become a sober young man; and he supposed that I would be free, on that account, to write it. We had much friendly talk on the subject, and then deferred it. A few days after, he came again, and directed their freedom; and so I wrote his will.

Near the time the last-mentioned Friend first spoke to me, a neighbor received a bad bruise in his body, and sent for me to bleed him; which being done, he desired me to write his will. I took notes; and amongst other things, he told me to which of his children he gave his young negro. I considered the pain and distress he was in, and knew not how it would end; so I wrote his will, save only that part concerning his slave, and carrying it to his bedside, read it to him, and then told him, in a friendly way, that I could not write any instrument by which my fellow-creatures were made slaves without bringing trouble on my mind. I let him know that I charged nothing for what I had done, and desired to be excused from doing the other part in the way he proposed: we then had a serious conference on the subject; and at length, he agreeing to set her free, I finished his will.

Having found drawings in my mind to visit Friends on Long Island, after obtaining a certificate from our Monthly Meeting, I set off on the 12th day of the fifth month, in the year 1756. When I reached the island, I lodged the first night at the house of my dear friend Richard Hallet. Next day being the first of the week, I was at the meeting in Newtown; in which we experienced the renewed manifestations of the love of Jesus Christ, to the comfort of the honest-hearted. I went that night to Flushing; and the next day, in company with my beloved friend Matthew Franklin, we crossed the ferry at White-stone; were at three meetings on the main, and then returned to the island, where I spent the remainder of the week in visiting meetings. The Lord, I believe, hath a people in those parts who are honestly inclined to serve him; but many, I fear, are too much clogged with the things of this life, and do not come forward, bearing the cross, in such faithfulness as he calls for.

My mind was deeply engaged in this visit, both in public and private; and at several places where I was, on observing that they had slaves, I found myself under a necessity, in a friendly way, to labor with them on that subject; expressing, as way opened, the inconsistency of that practice with the purity of the Christian religion, and the ill effects of it, manifested amongst us.

The latter end of the week, their Yearly Meeting began; at which were our friends John Scarborough, Jane Hoskins and

Susannah Brown, from Pennsylvania: the public meetings were large, and measurably favored with Divine goodness.

The exercise of my mind at this meeting, was chiefly on account of those who were considered as the foremost rank in the Society: and in a meeting of ministers and elders, way opened, so that I expressed in some measure what lay upon me; and at a time when Friends were met for transacting the affairs of the church, having sat awhile silent, I felt a weight on my mind, and stood up; and through the gracious regard of our heavenly Father, strength was given fully to clear myself of a burthen, which for some days had been increasing upon me.

Through the humbling dispensations of Divine Providence, men are sometimes fitted for his service. The messages of the prophet Jeremiah were so disagreeable to the people, and so reverse to the spirit they lived in, that he became the object of their reproach; and in the weakness of nature, thought of desisting from his prophetic office; but, saith he, "His word was in my heart as a burning fire shut up in my bones, and I was weary with forbearing, and could not stay." I saw at this time, that if I was honest in declaring that which Truth opened in me, I could not please all men; and labored to be content in the way of my duty, however disagreeable to my own inclination. After this I went homeward, taking Woodbridge and Plainfield in my way; in both which meetings, the pure influence of Divine love was manifested; in an humbling sense whereof I went home: having been out about twenty-four days, and rode about three hundred and sixteen miles.

While on this journey, my heart was much affected with a sense of the state of the churches in our southern provinces; and believing the Lord was calling me to some further labor amongst them, I was bowed in reverence before him, with fervent desires that I might find strength to resign myself to his heavenly will.

Until this year, 1756, I continued to retail goods, besides following my trade as a tailor; about which time I grew uneasy on account of my business growing too cumbersome. I had begun with selling trimmings for garments, and from thence proceeded to sell cloths and linens; and at length, having got a considerable shop of goods, my trade increased every year, and the road to large business appeared open; but I felt a stop in my mind.

Through the mercies of the Almighty, I had, in a good degree, learned to be content with a plain way of living; I had but a small family; and on serious consideration, I believed Truth did not require me to engage in many cumbering affairs. It had been my general practice to buy and sell things really useful; things that served chiefly to please the vain mind in people, I was not easy to trade in; seldom did it; and whenever I did, I found it to weaken me as a Christian.

The increase of business became my burthen; for though my natural inclination was toward merchandizing, yet I believed Truth required me to live more free from outward cumber; and there was now a strife in my mind between the two. In this exercise my prayers were put up to the Lord, who graciously heard me, and gave me a heart resigned to his holy will; then I lessened my business; and as I had opportunity, told my customers of my intentions, that they might consider what shop to turn to: and in a while, wholly laid down merchandise, following my trade as a tailor, myself only, having no apprentice. I also had a nursery of apple trees; in which I employed some of my time in hoeing, grafting, trimming, and inoculating. In merchandise it is the custom, where I lived, to sell chiefly on credit, and poor people often get in debt; and when payment is expected, not having wherewith to pay, their creditors often sue for it at law. Having often observed occurrences of this kind, I found it good for me to advise poor people to take such goods as were most useful and not costly.

In the time of trading, I had an opportunity of seeing that the too liberal use of spirituous liquors, and the custom of wearing too costly apparel, led some people into great inconveniences; and these two things appear to be often connected one with the other. By not attending to that use of things which is consistent with universal righteousness, there is an increase of labor, which extends beyond what our heavenly Father intends for us; by great labor, and often by much sweating, there is, even among such who are not drunkards, a craving of some liquors to revive the spirits; that, partly by the luxurious drinking of some, and partly by the drinking of others, led to it, through immoderate labor, very great quantities of rum are every year expended in our colonies; the greater part of which we should have no need of, did we steadily attend to pure wisdom.

Where men take pleasure in feeling their minds elevated with strong drink, and so indulge their appetite as to disorder their understandings, neglect their duty as members in a family or in civil society, and cast off all regard to religion, their case is much to be pitied; and where such whose lives are for the most part regular, and whose examples have a strong influence on the minds of others, adhere to some customs which powerfully draw to the use of more strong liquor than pure wisdom allows; this also, as it hinders the spreading of the spirit of meekness, and strengthens the hands of the more excessive drinkers, is a case to be lamented.

As every degree of luxury hath some connection with evil for those who profess to be disciples of Christ, and are looked upon as leaders of the people, to have that mind in them, which was also in Christ, and so stand separate from every wrong way, is a means of help to the weaker. As I have sometimes been much spent in the heat, and taken spirits to revive me, I have found by experience, that in such circumstances the mind is not so calm, nor so fitly disposed for Divine meditation, as when all such extremes are avoided; and I have felt an increasing care to attend to that holy Spirit which sets right bounds to our desires, and leads those who faithfully follow it, to apply all the gifts of Divine Providence to the purposes for which they were intended. Did such who have the care of great estates, attend with singleness of heart to this heavenly Instructor, which so opens and enlarges the mind, that men love their neighbors as themselves, they would have wisdom given them to manage, without finding occasion to employ some people in the luxuries of life, or to make it necessary for others to labor too hard; but for want of steadily regarding this principle of Divine love, a selfish spirit takes place in the minds of people, which is attended with darkness and manifold confusions in the world.

Though trading in things useful is an honest employ, yet, through the great number of superfluities which are bought and sold, and through the corruption of the times, they who apply to merchandize for a living have great need to be well experienced in that precept which the prophet Jeremiah laid down for his scribe: "Seekest thou great things for thyself? seek them not."

In the winter, this year, I was engaged with Friends in visiting families; and through the goodness of the Lord, we had oftentimes experience of his heart-tendering presence amongst us.

A copy of a letter written to a Friend.

In this thy late affliction I have found a deep fellow-feeling with thee; and had a secret hope throughout that it might please the Father of mercies to raise thee up, and sanctify thy troubles to thee; that thou, being more fully acquainted with that way which the world esteems foolish, may feel the clothing of Divine fortitude, and be strengthened to resist that spirit which leads from the simplicity of the everlasting Truth.

We may see ourselves crippled and halting, and, from a strong bias to things pleasant and easy, find an impossibility to advance; but things impossible with men are possible with God; and, our wills being made subject to his, all temptations are surmountable.

This work of subjecting the will is compared to the mineral in the furnace; which, through fervent heat, is reduced from its first principle: "He refines them as silver is refined — He shall sit as a refiner, and purifier of silver." By these comparisons, we are instructed in the necessity of the melting operation of the hand of God upon us, to prepare our hearts truly to adore him, and to manifest that adoration, by inwardly turning away from that spirit, in all its workings, which is not of him. To forward this work, the all-wise God is sometimes pleased, through outward distress, to bring us near the gates of death, that, life being painful and afflicting, and the prospect of eternity open before us, all earthly bonds may be loosened, and the mind prepared for that deep and sacred instruction which otherwise would not be received. If kind parents love their children, and delight in their happiness, then He, who is perfect goodness, in sending abroad mortal contagions, doth assuredly direct their use. Are the righteous removed by it, their change is happy; are the wicked taken away in their wickedness, the Almighty is clear. Do we pass through with anguish and great bitterness, and yet recover, He intends that we should be purged from dross, and our ear opened to discipline.

And now on thy part, after thy sore affliction and doubts of recovery, thou art again restored; forget not Him who hath helped thee, but in humble gratitude hold fast his instructions, thereby to shun those by-paths which lead from the firm foundation. I am sensible of that variety of company to which one in thy business must be exposed: I have painfully felt the force of conversation proceeding from men deeply rooted in an earthly mind, and can sympathize with others in such conflicts, in that much weakness still attends me.

I find that to be a fool as to worldly wisdom, and commit my cause to God, not fearing to offend men, who take offence at the simplicity of Truth, is the only way to remain unmoved at the sentiments of others.

The fear of man brings a snare; by halting in our duty, and giving back in the time of trial, our hands grow weaker, our spirits get mingled with the people, our ears grow dull as to hearing the language of the true Shepherd; so that when we look at the way of the righteous, it seems as though it was not for us to follow them.

There is a love clothes my mind while I write which is superior to all expressions; and I find my heart open to encourage to a holy emulation, to advance forward in Christian firmness. Deep humility is a strong bulwark; and as we enter into it, we find safety and true exaltation: the foolishness of God is wiser than man, and the weakness of God is stronger than man. Being unclothed of our own wisdom, and knowing the abasement of the creature, therein we find that power to arise which gives health and vigor to us.

CHAPTER IV

His visiting the families of Friends at Burlington — His journey to Pennsylvania, Maryland, Virginia, and North Carolina — Considerations on the state of Friends there, and the exercise he was under in travelling among those concerned in keeping slaves: with some observations on this subject — His epistle to Friends at New Garden and Cane Creek — His thoughts on the neglect of a religious care in the education of the negroes.

THE 13th day of the second month, in the year 1757, being then in good health, and abroad with Friends visiting families, I lodged at a Friend's house in Burlington; and going to bed about the time usual with me, I awoke in the night, and my meditations, as I lay, were on the goodness and mercy of the Lord; in a sense whereof my heart was contrite. After this, I went to sleep again; and sleeping a short time, I awoke. It was yet dark, and no appearance of day or moonshine; and as I opened mine eyes, I saw a light in my chamber at the apparent distance of five feet, about nine inches diameter, of a clear, easy brightness, and near its centre the most radiant. As I lay still, without any surprise, looking upon it, words were spoken to my inward ear, which filled my whole inward man: they were not the effect of thought, nor any conclusion in relation to the appearance, but as the language of the Holy One spoken in my mind: the words were, CERTAIN EVIDENCE OF DIVINE TRUTH; and were again repeated, exactly in the same manner; whereupon the light disappeared.

Feeling the exercise in relation to a visit to the southern provinces increase upon me, I acquainted our Monthly Meeting therewith, and obtained their certificate. Expecting to go alone,

one of my brothers, who lived in Philadelphia, having some business in North Carolina, proposed going with me part of the way; but as he had a view of some outward affairs, to accept of him as a companion seemed some difficulty with me. I had conversation with him at sundry times and at length, feeling easy in my mind, I had conversation with several elderly Friends of Philadelphia on the subject; and he obtaining a certificate suitable to the occasion, we set off in the fifth month of the year 1757. Coming to Nottingham week-day meeting, we lodged at John Churchman's, and here I met with our friend Benjamin Buffington, from New England, who was returning from a visit to the southern provinces. Thence we crossed the river Susquehanna, and lodged at William Cox's in Maryland; and soon after I entered this province, a deep and painful exercise came upon me, of which I had often had some feeling since my mind was drawn toward these parts, and with which I had acquainted my brother before we agreed to join as companions.

As the people in this and the southern provinces live much on the labor of slaves, many of whom are used hardly, my concern was, that I might attend with singleness of heart to the voice of the true Shepherd, and be so supported as to remain unmoved at the faces of men.

As it is common for Friends on such a visit to have entertainment free of cost, a difficulty arose in my mind with respect to saving my money by kindness received, which to me appeared to be the gain of oppression.

Receiving a gift, considered as a gift, brings the receiver under obligations to the benefactor, and has a natural tendency to draw the obliged into a party with the giver. To prevent difficulties of this kind, and to preserve the minds of judges from any bias, was that Divine prohibition; "Thou shalt not receive any gift: for a gift blindeth the wise, and perverteth the words of the righteous." As the disciples were sent forth without any provision for their journey, and our Lord said the workman is worthy of his meat, their labor in the Gospel was considered as a reward for their entertainment, and therefore not received as a gift; yet, in regard to my present journey, I could not see my way clear in that respect. The difference appeared thus: The entertainment the disciples met with, was from such whose hearts God had opened to receive them, from a love to them, and the truth they published. But we, considered as members of the same religious Society, look upon it as a piece of civility to receive each other in such visits; and such reception, at times, is partly in regard to reputation, and not from an inward unity of heart and spirit. Conduct is more convincing than language; and where people, by their actions, manifest that the slave-trade is not so disagreeable to their principles but that it may be encouraged, there is not a sound uniting with some Friends who visit them.

The prospect of so weighty a work, and being so distinguished from many whom I esteemed before myself, brought me very low; and such were the conflicts of my soul, that I had a near sympathy with the prophet, in the time of his weakness, when he said, "If thou deal thus with me, kill me, I pray thee, if I have found favor in thy sight"; but I soon saw that this proceeded from the want of a full resignation to the Divine will. Many were the afflictions which attended me; and in great abasement, with many tears, my cries were to the Almighty, for his gracious and fatherly assistance; and then, after a time of deep trial, I was favored to understand the state mentioned by the psalmist, more clearly than ever I had before; to wit: "My soul is even as a weaned child." Being thus helped to sink down into resignation, I felt a deliverance from that tempest in which I had been sorely exercised, and in calmness of mind went forward, trusting that the Lord Jesus Christ, as I faithfully attended to him, would be a counsellor to me in all difficulties; and that by his strength I should be enabled even to leave money with the members of Society where I had entertainment, when I found that omitting it would obstruct that work to which I believed he had called me. And as I copy this after my return, I may add, that oftentimes I did so, under a sense of duty. The way in which I did it was thus; when I expected soon to leave a Friend's house where I had had entertainment, if I believed that I should not keep clear from the gain of oppression without leaving money, I spoke to one of the heads of the family privately, and desired him to accept of some pieces of silver, and give them to such of the negroes as he believed would make the best use of them; and at other times I gave them to the negroes myself, as the way looked clearest to me. As I expected this before I came out, I had provided a large number of small pieces; and thus offering them to some who appeared to be wealthy people, was a trial both to me and them: but the fear of the Lord so covered me at times, that my way was made easier than I expected; and few, if any, manifested any resentment at the offer, and most of them, after some talk, accepted of them.

The 7th day of the fifth month, in the year 1757, I lodged at a Friend's house; and the next day being the first of the week, was at Patapsco meeting; then crossed Patuxent River, and lodged at a public house.

On the 9th, breakfasted at a Friend's house, who putting us a little on our way, I had conversation with him in the fear of the Lord, concerning his slaves; in which my heart was tender, and I used much plainness of speech with him, which he appeared to take kindly. We pursued our journey without appointing meetings, being pressed in my mind to be at the Yearly Meeting in Virginia. In my travelling on the road, I often felt a cry rise from the centre of my mind, O Lord, I am a stranger on the earth, hide not thy face from me. On the 11th day of the fifth month, we crossed the rivers Potomac and Rappahannock, and lodged at Port Royal: and on the way we happening in company with a colonel of the militia, who appeared to be a thoughtful man, I took occasion to remark on the difference in general between a people used to labor moderately for their living, training up their children in frugality and business, and those who live on the labor of slaves; the former, in my view, being the most happy life: with which he concurred, and mentioned the trouble arising from the untoward, slothful disposition of the negroes; adding, that one of our laborers would do as much in a day as two of their slaves. I replied, that free men, whose minds were properly on their business, found a satisfaction in improving, cultivating, and providing for their families; but negroes, laboring to support others, who claim them as their property, and expecting nothing but slavery during life, had not the like inducement to be industrious.

After some further conversation, I said that men having power, too often misapplied it; that though we made slaves of the negroes, and the Turks made slaves of the Christians, I believed that liberty was the natural right of all men equally; which he did not deny; but said the lives of the negroes were so wretched in their own country, that many of them lived better here than there. I only said there is great odds in regard to us, on what principle we act; and so the conversation on that subject ended. I may here add, that another person, some time afterward, mentioned the wretchedness of the negroes, occasioned by their intestine wars, as an argument in favor of our fetching them away for slaves; to which I then replied, if compassion on the Africans, in regard to their domestic troubles, were the real motives of our purchasing them, that spirit of tenderness being attended to, would incite us to use them kindly, that as strangers brought out of affliction, their lives might be happy among us; and as they are human creatures, whose souls are as precious as ours, and who may receive the same help and comfort from the holy Scriptures as we do, we could not omit suitable endeavors to instruct them therein. But while we manifest by our conduct, that our views in purchasing them are to advance ourselves; and while our buying captives taken in war, animates those parties to push on that war, and increase desolation amongst them; to say they live unhappily in Africa, is far from being an argument in our favor. I further said, the present circumstances of these provinces to me appear difficult; the slaves look like a burthensome stone to such who burthen themselves with them, and that if the white people retain a resolution to prefer their outward prospects of gain to all other considerations, and do not act conscientiously toward them as fellow-creatures, I believe that burthen will grow heavier and heavier, until times change in a way disagreeable to us. At this the person appeared very serious, and owned, that in considering their condition, and the manner of their treatment in these provinces, he had sometimes thought it might be just in the Almighty so to order it.

Having travelled through Maryland, we came amongst Friends at Cedar Creek, in Virginia, on the 12th day of the fifth month; and the next day rode, in company with several Friends, a day's journey to Camp Creek. As I was riding along in the morning, my mind was deeply affected in a sense I had of the want of Divine aid to support me in the various difficulties which attended me; and in an uncommon distress of mind, I cried in secret to the Most High, Oh, Lord! be merciful, I beseech thee, to thy poor afflicted creature. After some time, I felt inward relief; and soon after, a Friend in company began to talk in support of the slave-trade, and said the negroes were understood to be the offspring of Cain, their blackness being the mark God set upon him after he murdered Abel, his brother, and that it was the design of Providence they should be slaves, as a condition proper to the race of so wicked a man as Cain was. Then another spake in support of what had been said. To all which, I replied in substance as follows: that Noah and his family were all who survived the flood, according to Scripture; and as Noah's was of Seth's race, the family of Cain was wholly destroyed. One of them said, that after the flood Ham went to the land of Nod, and took a wife; that Nod was a land far distant, inhabited by Cain's race, and that the flood did not reach it; and as Ham was sentenced to be a servant of servants to his brethren, these two families, being thus joined, were undoubtedly fit only for slaves. I replied, the flood was a judgment upon the world for their abominations; and it was granted that Cain's stock was the most wicked, and therefore unreasonable to suppose they were spared: as to Ham's going to the land of Nod for a wife, no time being fixed, Nod might be inhabited by some of Noah's family before Ham married a second time; moreover, the text saith, "That all flesh died that moved upon the earth." I further reminded them how the prophets repeatedly declare "that the son shall not suffer for the iniquity of the father; but every one be answerable for his own sins." I was troubled to perceive the darkness of their imaginations; and in some pressure of spirit, said, the love of ease and gain are the motives in general of keeping slaves, and men are wont to take hold of weak arguments to support a cause which is unreasonable; and added, I have no interest on either side, save only the interest which I desire to have in the Truth; and as I believe liberty is their right, and see they are not only deprived of it, but treated in other respects with inhumanity in many places, I believe He, who is a refuge for the oppressed, will in his own time plead their cause; and happy will it be for such who walk in uprightness before him. Thus our conversation ended.

On the 14th day of the fifth month I was at Camp Creek Monthly Meeting, and then rode to the mountains of James River, and had a meeting at a Friend's house; in both of which I felt sorrow of heart, and my tears were poured out before the Lord, who was pleased to afford a degree of strength by which way was opened to clear my mind amongst Friends in those places. From thence I went to Fork Creek, and so to Cedar Creek again; at which place I now had a meeting. Here I found a tender seed; and as I was preserved in the ministry to keep low with the Truth, the same Truth in their hearts answered it, so that it was a time of mutual refreshment from the presence of the Lord. I lodged at James Stanley's, father of William Stanley, one of the young men who suffered imprisonment at Winchester last summer, on account of their testimony against fighting; and I had some satisfactory conversation with him concerning it. Hence I went to the Swamp and Wainoak meetings; and then crossed James River, and lodged near Burleigh. From the time of my entering Maryland I have been much under sorrow, which of late so increased upon me, that my mind was almost overwhelmed; and I may say with the psalmist, "In my distress I called upon the Lord, and cried to my God"; who, in infinite goodness, looked upon my affliction, and in my private retirement sent the Comforter for my relief; for which I humbly bless his holy name.

The sense I had of the state of the churches brought a weight of distress upon me; the gold to me appeared dim, and the fine gold changed: and though this is the case too generally, yet the sense of it in these parts hath, in a particular manner, borne heavily upon me. It appeared to me that, through the prevailing of the spirit of this world, the minds of many were brought to inward desolation; and instead of the spirit of meekness, gentleness, and heavenly wisdom, which are the necessary companions of the true sheep of Christ, a spirit of fierceness and the love of dominion too generally prevailed. From small beginnings in error, great buildings, by degrees, are raised; and from one age to another are more and more strengthened by the general concurrence of the people. As men obtain reputation by their profession of the Truth, their virtues are mentioned as arguments in favor of general error; and those of less note, to justify themselves, say such and such good men did the like. By what other steps could the people of Judah rise to that height in wickedness as to give just ground for the prophet Isaiah to declare in the name of the Lord, "that none calleth for justice, nor any pleadeth for truth": or for the Almighty to call upon the great city of Jerusalem, just before the Babylonish captivity, "If ye can find a man, if there be any who executeth judgment, that seeketh the Truth, and I will pardon it." The prospect of a road lying open to the same degeneracy, in some parts of this newly settled land of America, in respect to our conduct toward the negroes, hath deeply bowed my mind in this journey; and though to relate briefly how these people are treated is no agreeable work, yet, after often reading over the notes I made as I travelled, I find my mind engaged to preserve them. Many of the white people in those provinces take little or no care of negro marriages; and when negroes marry after their own way, some make so little account of those marriages, that, with views of outward interest, they often part men from their wives by selling them far asunder; which is common when estates are sold by executors at vendue. Many whose labor is heavy being followed at their business in the field by a man with a whip, hired for that purpose, having in common little else allowed but one peck of Indian corn and some salt for one week, with a few potatoes; the potatoes they commonly raise by their labor on the first day of the week.

The correction ensuing on their disobedience to overseers, or slothfulness in business, is often very severe, and sometimes desperate.

Men and women have many times scarcely clothes enough to hide their nakedness, and boys and girls, ten and twelve years old, are often quite naked amongst their master's children. Some of our Society, and some of the society called New Lights, use some endeavors to instruct those they have in reading; but in common this is not only neglected, but disapproved. These are the people by whose labor the other inhabitants are in a great measure supported, and many of them in the luxuries of life; these are the people who have made no agreement to serve us, and who have not forfeited their liberty, that we know of; these are the souls for whom Christ died: and for our conduct toward them, we must answer before Him who is no respecter of persons.

They who know the only true God, and Jesus Christ, whom he hath sent, and are thus acquainted with the merciful, benevolent, Gospel spirit, will therein perceive that the indignation of God is kindled against oppression and cruelty; and in beholding the great distress of so numerous a people, will find cause for mourning.

From my lodgings I went to Burleigh meeting, where I felt my mind drawn into a quiet, resigned state; and after a long silence, I felt an engagement to stand up; and through the powerful operation of Divine love, we were favored with an edifying meeting. The next meeting we had was at Black Water; and so to the Yearly Meeting at the Western Branch. When its business began, some queries were considered by some of their members, to be now produced; and if approved, to be answered hereafter by their respective Monthly Meetings. They were the Pennsylvania queries, which had been examined by a committee of Virginia Yearly Meeting, appointed last year, who made some alterations in them; one of which alterations was made in favor of a custom which troubled me. The query was, "Are there any concerned in the importation of negroes, or buying them after imported?" which they altered thus: "Are there any concerned in the importation of negroes, or buying them to trade in?" As one query admitted with unanimity was, "Are any concerned in buying or vending goods unlawfully imported, or prize goods?" I found my mind engaged to say, that, as we professed the Truth, and were there assembled to support the testimony of it, it was necessary for us to dwell deep, and act in that wisdom which is pure, or otherwise we could not prosper. I then mention the alteration; and referring to the last-mentioned query, added, as purchasing any merchandize taken by the sword was always allowed to be inconsistent with the principles, negroes being captives of war, or taken by stealth, those circumstances make it inconsistent with our testimony to buy them; and their being our fellow-creatures who are sold as slaves, adds greatly to the iniquity. Friends appeared attentive to what was said; some expressed a care and concern about their negroes; none made any objection by way of reply to what I said; but the query was admitted as they had altered it. As some of their members have heretofore traded in negroes, as in other merchandize, this query being admitted will be one step further than they have hitherto gone. I did not see it my duty to press for an alteration; but felt easy to leave it all to Him, who alone is able to turn the hearts of the mighty, and to make way for the spreading of Truth on the earth by means agreeable to his infinite wisdom. But in regard to those they already had, I felt my mind engaged to labor with them; and said that, as we believe the Scriptures were given forth by holy men as they were moved by the Holy Ghost, and many of us know by experience that they are often helpful and comfortable, and believing ourselves bound in duty to teach our children to read them, I believe that if we were divested of all selfish views, the same good Spirit that gave them forth would engage us to teach the negroes to read, that they might have the benefit of them: there were some amongst them who, at this time, manifested a concern in regard to taking more care in the education of their negroes.

On the 29th day of the fifth month, at the house where I lodged was a meeting of ministers and elders, at the ninth hour in the morning; at which time I found an engagement to speak freely and plainly to them concerning their slaves; mentioning how they, as the first rank in the Society, whose conduct in that case was much noticed by others, were under the stronger obligations to look carefully to themselves: expressing how needful it was for them, in that situation, to be thoroughly divested of all selfish views; that living in the pure Truth, and acting conscientiously toward those people in their education and otherwise, they might be instrumental in helping forward a work so exceedingly necessary, and so much neglected amongst them. At the twelfth hour the meeting for worship began, which was solid.

On the 30th day, about the tenth hour, Friends met to finish their business, and then the meeting for worship ensued, which to me was a laborious time; but through the goodness of the Lord, Truth, I believed, gained some ground; and it was a strengthening opportunity to the honest-hearted.

About this time I wrote an epistle to Friends in the back settlements of North Carolina, as follows:—

To Friends at their Monthly Meeting at New Garden and Cane Creek, in North Carolina.

Dear Friends,

It having pleased the Lord to draw me forth on a visit to some parts of Virginia and Carolina, you have often been in my mind; and though my way is not clear to come in person to visit you, yet I feel it in my heart to communicate a few things, as they arise in the love of Truth. First, my dear Friends, dwell in humility; and take heed that no views of outward gain get too deep hold of you, that so your eyes being single to the Lord, you may be preserved in the way of safety. Where people let loose their minds after the love of outward things, and are more engaged in pursuing the profits and seeking the friendships of this world, than to be inwardly acquainted with the way of true peace, such walk in a vain shadow, while the true comfort of life is wanting: their examples are often hurtful to others; and their treasures, thus collected, do many times prove dangerous snares to their children.

But where people are sincerely devoted to follow Christ, and dwell under the influence of his holy Spirit, their stability and firmness, through a Divine blessing, is at times like dew on the tender plants around about them, and the weightiness of their spirits secretly works on the minds of others; and in this condition, through the spreading influence of Divine love, they feel a care over the flock; and way is opened for maintaining good order in the Society. And though we meet with opposition from another spirit, yet, as there is a dwelling in meekness, feeling our spirits subject, and moving only in the gentle peaceable wisdom, the inward reward of quietness, will be greater than all our difficulties. Where the pure life is kept to, and meetings of discipline are held in the authority of it, we find by experience that they are comfortable, and tend to the health of the body.

While I write, the youth come fresh in my way. — Dear young people, choose God for your portion; love his Truth, and be not ashamed of it; choose for your company such who serve him in uprightness; and shun, as most dangerous, the conversation of those whose lives are of an ill savour; for by frequenting such company, some hopeful young people have come to great loss, and been drawn from less evils to greater to their utter ruin. In the bloom of youth no ornament is so lovely as that of virtue, nor any enjoyments equal to those which we partake of, in fully resigning ourselves to the Divine will. These enjoyments add sweetness to all other comforts, and give true satisfaction in company and conversation, where people are mutually acquainted with it; and as your minds are thus seasoned with the Truth, you will find strength to abide steadfast to the testimony of it, and be prepared for services in the church.

And now, dear friends and brethren, as you are improving a wilderness, and may be numbered amongst the first planters in one part of a province, I beseech you, in the love of Jesus Christ, wisely to consider the force of your examples, and think how much your successors may be thereby affected. It is a help in a country, yea, a great favor and a blessing, when customs first settled, are agreeable to sound wisdom; so when they are otherwise, the effect of them is grievous; and children feel themselves encompassed with difficulties prepared for them by their predecessors.

As moderate care and exercise, under the direction of true wisdom, is useful both to mind and body; so by this means in general, the real wants of life are easily supplied; our gracious Father having so proportioned one to the other, that, keeping in the true medium, we may pass on quietly. Where slaves are purchased to do our labor, numerous difficulties attend. To rational creatures bondage is uneasy, and frequently occasions sourness and discontent in them; which affects the family, and such who claim the mastery over them: and thus people and their children are many times encompassed with vexations, which arise from their applying to wrong methods to get a living.

I have been informed that there are a large number of Friends in your parts, who have no slaves; and in tender and most affectionate love, I beseech you to keep clear from purchasing any. Look, my dear friends, to Divine Providence; and follow in simplicity that exercise of body, that plainness and frugality, which true wisdom leads to; so may you be preserved from those dangers which attend such who are aiming at outward ease and greatness.

Treasures, though small, attained on the true principle of virtue, are sweet in the possession; and while we walk in the light of the Lord, there is true comfort and satisfaction. Here, neither the murmurs of an oppressed people, nor the throbbings of an uneasy conscience, nor anxious thoughts about the event of things, hinder the enjoyment of life.

When we look toward the end of life, and think on the division of our substance among our successors, if we know that it was collected in the fear of the Lord, in honesty, in equity, and in uprightness of heart before him, we may consider it as his gift to us; and with a single eye to his blessing, bestow it on those we leave behind us. Such is the happiness of the plain way of true virtue. "The work of righteousness shall be peace; and the effect of righteousness, quietness, and assurance for ever."

Dwell here, my dear Friends; and then in remote and solitary deserts, you may find true peace and satisfaction. If the Lord be our God, in truth and reality, there is safety for us; for he is a strong hold in the day of trouble, and knoweth them that trust in him.

Isle of Wight county, in Virginia,
29th of the fifth month, 1757.

From the Yearly Meeting in Virginia, I went to Carolina; and on the 1st day of the sixth month, was at Wells Monthly Meeting, where the spring of the Gospel ministry was opened, and the love of Jesus Christ experienced amongst us: to his name be the praise.

Here my brother joined with some friends from New Garden, who were going homeward; and I went next to Simons Creek Monthly Meeting, where I was silent during the meeting for worship. When business came on, my mind was exercised concerning the poor slaves; but I did not feel my way clear to speak; in this condition I was bowed in spirit before the Lord; and with tears and inward supplication besought him, so to open my understanding, that I might know his will concerning me; and at length, my mind was settled in silence. Near the end of their business, a member of the meeting expressed a concern, that had some time lain upon him, on account of Friends so much neglecting their duty in the education of their slaves, and proposed having meetings sometimes appointed for them on a week-day, to be only attended by some Friends to be named in their Monthly Meetings. Many present appeared to unite with the proposal: one said he had often wondered that they, being our fellow-creatures and capable of religious understanding, had been so exceedingly neglected: another expressed the like concern, and appeared zealous that Friends in future, might more closely consider it: at length a minute was made; and the further consideration of it referred to their next Monthly Meeting. The Friend who made this proposal has negroes: he told me that he was at New Garden; about two hundred and fifty miles from home, and came back alone; and that in this solitary journey, this exercise in regard to the education of their negroes, was, from time to time, renewed in his mind. A Friend of some note in Virginia, who has slaves, told me, that he being far from home on a lonesome journey, had many serious thoughts about them; and that his mind was so impressed therewith, that he believed he saw a time coming, when Divine Providence would alter the circumstances of these people, respecting their condition as slaves.

From hence I went to Newbegun Creek, and sat a considerable time in much weakness; then I felt Truth open the way to speak a little in much plainness and simplicity, till, at length, through the increase of Divine love amongst us, we had a seasoning opportunity. From thence I went to the head of Little river, where was, on a first-day, a crowded meeting; and I believe, through Divine goodness, it was made profitable to some. — Thence to the Old Neck; where I was led into a careful searching out the secret workings of the mystery of iniquity, which, under a cover of religion, exalts itself against that pure spirit, which leads in the way of meekness and self-denial. From thence to Piney-woods; which was the last meeting I was at in Carolina, and was large; and my heart being deeply engaged, I was drawn forth in fervent labor amongst them.

When I was at Newbegun Creek, a Friend was there who labored for his living, having no negroes, and had been a minister many years. He came to me the next day, and as we rode together, signified that he wanted to talk with me concerning a difficulty he had been under, and related it nearly as follows: to wit, That as moneys had been raised by a tax of late years to carry on war, he had a scruple in his mind in regard to paying it, and chose rather to suffer distraint of his goods than pay it°; and as he was the only person who refused it in those parts, and knew not that any one else was in the like circumstances, he signified that it had been a heavy trial to him, and more so, for that some of his brethren had been uneasy with his conduct in that case. He added, that from a sympathy he felt with me yesterday in meeting, he found freedom thus to open the matter, in the way of query concerning Friends in our parts. I told him the state of Friends amongst us, as well as I was able; and also, that I had for some time been under the like scruple. I believed him to be one who was concerned to walk uprightly before the Lord; and esteemed it my duty to preserve this note concerning him; his name was Samuel Newby.

From hence I went back into Virginia, and had a meeting near James Cowplands; it was a time of inward suffering; but through the goodness of the Lord, I was made content: then to another meeting; where, through the renewings of pure love, we had a very comfortable season.

Travelling up and down of late, I have had renewed evidences, that to be faithful to the Lord and contented with his will concerning me, is a most necessary and useful lesson for me to be learning; looking less at the effects of my labor, than at the pure motion and reality of the concern, as it arises from heavenly love. In the Lord Jehovah is everlasting strength; and as the mind, by humble resignation, is united to him, and we utter words from an inward knowledge that they arise from the heavenly spring, though our way may be difficult, and require close attention to keep in it; and though the manner in which we may be led may tend to our own abasement; yet, if we continue in patience and meekness, heavenly peace is the reward of our labors.

From thence I went to Curles meeting; which, though small, was reviving to the honest-hearted. Thence to Black Creek and Caroline meetings; from whence, accompanied by William Stanley, before mentioned, we rode to Goose creek, being much through the woods, and about one hundred miles. We lodged the first night at a public house; the second in the woods; and the next day we reached a Friend's house, at Goose creek. In the woods we lay under some disadvantage, having no fire-works nor bells for our horses; but we stopped a little before night, and let them feed on the wild grass which was plenty; in the mean time cutting with our knives a store against night, and then tied them; and gathering some bushes under an oak, we lay down; but the mosquitoes being plenty and the ground damp, I slept but little. Lying in the wilderness, and looking at the stars, I was led to contemplate the condition of our first parents, when they were sent forth from the garden; but the Almighty, though they had been disobedient, continued to be a Father to them, and showed them what tended to their felicity as intelligent creatures, and was acceptable to him. To provide things relative to our outward living, in the way of true wisdom is good; and the gift of improving in things useful is a good gift, and comes from the Father of lights. Many have had this gift; and from age to age, there having been improvements of this kind made in the world: but some not keeping to the pure gift, have, in the creaturely cunning and self-exaltation, sought out many inventions; which inventions of men, distinct from that uprightness in which man was created, as the first motion to them was evil, so the effects have been and are evil. At this day, it is as necessary for us constantly to attend on the heavenly gift, to be qualified to use rightly the good things in this life amidst great improvements, as it was for our first parents, when they were without any improvements, without any friend or father but God only.

I was at a meeting at Goose Creek; and next at a Monthly Meeting at Fairfax; where, through the gracious dealing of the Almighty with us, his power prevailed over many hearts. Thence to Manoquacy and Pipe Creek, in Maryland; at both which places I had cause humbly to adore Him, who supported me through many exercises, and by whose help I was enabled to reach the true witness in the hearts of others: there were some hopeful young people in those parts. I had meetings at John Everit's in Monallen, and at Huntingdon; and was made humbly thankful to the Lord, who opened my heart amongst the people in these new settlements, so that it was a time of encouragement to the honest-minded.

At Monallen, a Friend gave me some account of a religious society among the Dutch, called Mennonists°; and amongst other things, related a passage in substance as follows: — One of the Mennonists having acquaintance with a man of another society at a considerable distance, and being with his wagon on business near the house of his said acquaintance, and night coming on, he had thoughts of putting up with him; but passing by his fields, and observing the distressed appearance of his slaves, he kindled a fire in the woods hard by, and lay there that night. His acquaintance hearing where he lodged, and afterward meeting the Mennonist, told him of it; adding, he should have been heartily welcome at his house; and from their acquaintance in former time, he wondered at his conduct in that case. The Mennonist replied, ever since I lodged by thy field, I have wanted an opportunity to speak with thee. I intended to come to thy house for entertainment, but seeing thy slaves at their work, and observing the manner of their dress I had no liking to come to partake with thee; he then admonished him to use them with more humanity, and added, as I lay by the fire that night, I thought that as I was a man of substance, thou wouldst have received me freely; but if I had been as poor as one of thy slaves, and had no power to help myself, I should have received from thy hand no kinder usage than they.

From hence I was at three meetings in my way, and so went home, under an humbling sense of the gracious dealings of the Lord with me, in preserving me through many trials and afflictions in my journey. I was out about two months, and travelled about eleven hundred and fifty miles.

CHAPTER V

Considerations on the payment of a tax laid for carrying on the war against the Indians — Some notes on Thomas à Kempis and John Huss — Meetings of the committee of the Yearly Meeting at Philadelphia — The present circumstances of Friends in Pennsylvania and New Jersey very different from those of our predecessors — The drafting of the militia in New Jersey to serve in the army, with some observations on the state of the members of our Society at that time — His visit to Friends in Pennsylvania, accompanied by Benjamin Jones — Proceedings at the Monthly, Quarterly, and Yearly Meetings in Philadelphia, respecting those who keep slaves.

A FEW years past, money being made current in our province for carrying on wars, and to be called in again by taxes laid on the inhabitants, my mind was often affected with the thoughts of paying such taxes; and I believe it right for me to preserve a memorandum concerning it. I was told, that Friends in England frequently paid taxes, when the money was applied to such purposes. I had conversation with several noted Friends on the subject, who all favored the payment of such taxes; some of whom I preferred before myself, and this made me easier for a time; yet there was in the deeps of my mind, a scruple which I never could get over; and at certain times, I was greatly distressed on that account.

I all along believed that there were some upright-hearted men, who paid such taxes; but could not see that their example was a sufficient reason for me to do so, while I believed that the Spirit of Truth required of me, as an individual, to suffer patiently the distress of goods, rather than pay actively.

I have been informed that Thomas à Kempis° lived and died in the profession of the Roman Catholic religion · and in reading his writings, I have believed him to be a man of a true Christian spirit; as fully so, as many who died martyrs because they could not join with some superstitions in that church.

All true Christians are of the same spirit, but their gifts are diverse; Jesus Christ appointing to each one their peculiar office, agreeably to his infinite wisdom.

John Huss° contended against the errors crept into the church, in opposition to the council of Constance; which the historian reports to have consisted of some thousand persons. He modestly vindicated the cause which he believed was right; and though his language and conduct toward his judges appear to have been respectful, yet he never could be moved from the principles settled in his mind. To use his own words: "This I most humbly require and desire of you all, even for his sake who is the God of us all, that I be not compelled to the thing which my conscience doth repugn or strive against."—And again, in his answer to the emperor: "I refuse nothing, most noble emperor, whatsoever the council shall decree or determine upon me, only this one thing I except, that I do not offend God and my conscience."° Fox's Acts and Monuments, page 233. At length, rather than act contrary to that which he believed the Lord required of him, he chose to suffer death by fire. Thomas à Kempis, without disputing against the articles then generally agreed to, appears to have labored, by a pious example as well as by preaching and writing, to promote virtue and the inward spiritual religion: and I believe they were both sincere-hearted followers of Christ.

True charity is an excellent virtue: and to labor sincerely for their good, whose beliefs, in all points, do not agree with ours, is a happy state. To refuse the active payment of a tax which our Society generally paid, was exceedingly disagreeable;

but to do a thing contrary to my conscience, appeared yet more dreadful. When this exercise came upon me, I knew of none under the like difficulty; and in my distress, I besought the Lord to enable me to give up all, that so I might follow him wheresoever he was pleased to lead me. Under this exercise I went to our Yearly Meeting at Philadelphia, in the year 1755; at which a committee was appointed of some from each quarter, to correspond with the Meeting for Sufferings in London; and another to visit our Monthly and Quarterly Meetings; and after their appointment, before the last adjournment of the meeting, it was agreed that these two committees should meet together in Friends' school-house in the city, at a time then concluded on, to consider some things in which the cause of Truth was concerned. These committees meeting together, had a weighty conference in the fear of the Lord; at which time, I perceived there were many Friends under a scruple like that before-mentioned.°

As scrupling to pay a tax on account of the application, hath seldom been heard of heretofore, even amongst men of integrity, who have steadily borne their testimony against war, in their time; I may here note some things which have occurred to my mind, as I have been inwardly exercised on that account. From the steady opposition which faithful Friends, in early times, made to wrong things then approved of, they were hated and persecuted by men living in the spirit of this world; and suffering with firmness, they were made a blessing to the church, and the work prospered. It equally concerns men in every age, to take heed to their own spirit; and in comparing their situation with ours, it looks to me that there was less danger of their being infected with the spirit of this world, in paying such taxes, than there is of us now. They had little or no share in civil government; and many of them declared, they were, through the power of God, separated from the spirit in which wars were; and being afflicted by the rulers on account of their testimony, there was less likelihood of uniting in spirit with them in things inconsistent with the purity of Truth. We, from the first settlement of this land, have known little or no troubles of that sort. Their profession for a time, was accounted reproachful; but at length, the uprightness of our predecessors being understood by the rulers, and their innocent sufferings moving them, our way of worship was tolerated; and many of our members in these colonies became active in civil government. Being thus tried with favor and prosperity, this world hath appeared inviting; our minds have been turned to the improvement of our country, to merchandize and sciences, amongst which are many things useful, being followed in pure wisdom; but in our present condition, that a carnal mind is gaining upon us, I believe will not be denied. Some of our members, who are officers in civil government, are, in one case or other, called upon in their respective stations to assist in things relative to the wars. Such being in doubt whether to act, or craved to be excused from their office, seeing their brethren united in the payment of a tax to carry on the said wars, might think their case not much different, and so quench the tender movings of the Holy Spirit in their minds; and thus, by small degrees, there might be an approach toward fighting, until we came so near it, as that the distinction would be little else but the name of a peaceable people.

It requires great self-denial and resignation of ourselves to God, to attain that state wherein we can freely cease from fighting when wrongfully invaded, if by our fighting there was a probability of overcoming the invaders. — Whoever rightly attains to it, does, in some degree, feel that spirit in which our Redeemer gave his life for us; and through Divine goodness, many of our predecessors, and many now living, have learned this blessed lesson. But many others, having their religion chiefly by education, and not being enough acquainted with that cross which crucifies to the world, manifest a temper distinguishable from that of an entire trust in God. In calmly considering these things, it hath not appeared strange to me, that an exercise hath now fallen upon some, which, as to the outward means of it, is different from what was known to many of those who went before us.

Some time after the Yearly Meeting, a day being appointed and letters written to distant members, the said committees met at Philadelphia; and by adjournments, continued several days. The calamities of war were now increasing; the frontier inhabitants of Pennsylvania were frequently surprised, some slain, and many taken captive by the Indians; and while these committees sat, the corpse of one so slain was brought in a wagon, and taken through the streets of the city, in his bloody garments, to alarm the people, and rouse them up to war.

Friends thus met were not all of one mind in relation to the tax; which, to such who scrupled it, made the way more difficult. To refuse an active payment at such a time, might be construed into an act of disloyalty, and appeared likely to displease the rulers, not only here but in England. Still there was a scruple so fastened upon the minds of many Friends, that nothing moved it: it was a conference the most weighty that ever I was at, and the hearts of many were bowed in reverence before the Most High. Some Friends of the said committees who appeared easy to pay the tax, after several adjournments, withdrew, others of them continued till the last. At length, an epistle of tender love and caution to Friends in Pennsylvania, was drawn by some Friends concerned, on that subject; and being read several times and corrected, was then signed by such of them as were free to sign it, and afterwards sent to the Monthly and Quarterly Meetings.

On the 9th day of the eighth month, in the year 1757, at night, orders came to the military officers in our county, (Burlington), directing them to draft the militia and prepare a number of men to go as soldiers, to the relief of the English at fort William Henry,° in New York government. A few days after, there was a general review of the militia at Mount Holly, and a number of men chosen and sent off under some officers. Shortly after, there came orders to draft three times as many, to hold themselves in readiness to march when fresh orders came; and on the 17th day of the eighth month, there was a meeting of the military officers at Mount Holly, who agreed on a draft, and orders were sent to the men so chosen, to meet their respective captains at set times and places; those in our township to meet at Mount Holly; amongst whom were a considerable number of our Society. My mind being affected herewith, I had fresh opportunity to see and consider the advantage of living in the real substance of religion where practice doth harmonize with principle. Amongst the officers are men of understanding, who have some regard to sincerity where they see it; and in the execution of their office, when they have men to deal with whom they believe to be upright-hearted, to put them to trouble on account of scruples of conscience, is a painful task, and likely to be avoided as much as easily may be. But where men profess to be so meek and heavenly-minded, and to have their trust so firmly settled in God, that they cannot join in wars; and yet, by their spirit and conduct in common life, manifest a contrary disposition, their difficulties are great at such a time.

Officers, who, in great anxiety, are endeavoring to get troops to answer the demands of their superiors, seeing men who are insincere, pretend a scruple of conscience, in hopes of being excused from a dangerous employment, are likely to handle them roughly. In this time of commotion some of our young men left the parts, and tarried abroad till it was over; some came and proposed to go as soldiers; others appeared to have a real tender scruple in their minds against joining in wars, and were much humbled under the apprehension of a trial so near. I had conversation with several of these to my satisfaction. At the set time when the captain came to town, some of those last-mentioned went and told him in substance as follows: — That they could not bear arms for conscience' sake; nor could they hire any to go in their places, being resigned as to the event of it: at length the captain acquainted them all, that they might return home for the present, and required them to provide themselves as soldiers, and to be in readiness to march when called upon. This was such a time as I had not seen before; and yet I may say, with thankfulness to the Lord, that I believed this trial was intended for our good; and I was favored with resignation to him. The French army taking the fort they were besieging, destroyed it and went away: the company of men first drafted, after some days' march, had orders to return home; and those on the second draft were no more called upon on that occasion.

On the 4th day of the fourth month, in the year 1758, orders came to some officers in Mount Holly, to prepare quarters a short time, for about one hundred soldiers: an officer and two other men, all inhabitants of our town, came to my house; and the officer told me that he came to speak with me, to provide lodging and entertainment for two soldiers, there being six shillings a week per man allowed as pay for it. The case being new and unexpected, I made no answer suddenly; but sat a time silent, my mind being turned inward. I was fully convinced, that the proceedings in wars are inconsistent with the purity of the Christian religion: and to be hired to entertain men, who were then under pay as soldiers, was a difficulty with me. I expected they had legal authority for what they did; and after a short time, I said to the officer, if the men are sent here for entertainment, I believe I shall not refuse to admit them into my house; but the nature of the case is such, that I expect I cannot keep them on hire: one of the men intimated, that he thought I might do it consistently with my religious principles; to which I made no reply, believing silence, at that time, best for me. Though they spoke of two, there came only one, who tarried at my house about two weeks, and behaved himself civilly; and when the officer came to pay me, I told him I could not take pay for it, having admitted him into my house in passive obedience to authority. I was on horseback when he spoke to me; and as I turned from him, he said, he was obliged to me: to which I said nothing; but thinking on the expression, I grew uneasy; and afterwards being near where he lived, I went and told him on what grounds I refused taking pay for keeping the soldier.

Near the beginning of the year 1758, I went one evening in company with a Friend, to visit a sick person; and before our return, we were told of a woman living near, who, of late, had been disconsolate several days, occasioned by a dream, wherein death, and the judgments of the Almighty after death, were represented to her mind in a moving manner. Her sadness on that account being worn off, the Friend with whom I was in company went to see her, and had some religious conversation with her and her husband: with this visit they were somewhat affected; and the man, with many tears expressed his satisfaction: and in a short time after, the poor man being on the river in a storm of wind, he with one more was drowned.

In the eighth month of the year 1758, having had drawings in my mind to be at the Quarterly Meeting in Chester county, and at some meetings in the county of Philadelphia, I went first to the said Quarterly Meeting, which was large; and several weighty matters came under consideration and debate; and the Lord was pleased to qualify some of his servants with strength and firmness, to bear the burthen of the day. Though I said but little, my mind was deeply exercised; and under a sense of God's love, in anointing and fitting some young men for his work, I was comforted, and my heart was tendered before him. From hence I went to the Youths' meeting at

Darby, where my beloved friend and brother Benjamin Jones met me, by an appointment before I left home, to join in the visit. We were at Radnor, Merion, Richland, North Wales, Plymouth, and Abington meetings; and had cause to bow in reverence before the Lord our gracious God, by whose help way was opened for us from day to day. I was out about two weeks, and rode about two hundred miles.

The Monthly Meeting of Philadelphia having been under a concern on account of some Friends, who this summer, 1758, had bought negro slaves; the said meeting moved it to their Quarterly Meeting, to have the minute reconsidered in the Yearly Meeting, which was made last on that subject. The said Quarterly Meeting appointed a committee to consider it, and report to their next; which committee having met once and adjourned, and I going to Philadelphia to meet a committee of the Yearly Meeting, was in town the evening on which the Quarterly Meeting's committee met the second time; and finding an inclination to sit with them, was with some others admitted; and Friends had a weighty conference on the subject. Soon after their next Quarterly Meeting, I heard that the case was coming to our Yearly Meeting; which brought a weighty exercise upon me, and under a sense of my own infirmities, and the great danger I felt of turning aside from perfect purity, my mind was often drawn to retire alone, and put my prayers to the Lord, that he would be graciously pleased to strengthen me; that setting aside all views of self-interest and the friendship of this world, I might stand fully resigned to his holy will.

In this Yearly Meeting several weighty matters were considered; and toward the last, that in relation to dealing with persons who purchase slaves. During the several sittings of the said meeting, my mind was frequently covered with inward prayer; and I could say with David, "that tears were my meat day and night." The case of slave-keeping lay heavy upon me; nor did I find any engagement to speak directly to any other matter before the meeting. When this case was opened, several faithful friends spoke weightily thereto, with which I was comforted; and feeling a concern to cast in my mite, I said in substance, as follows: —

"In the difficulties attending us in this life, nothing is more precious than the mind of Truth inwardly manifested; and it is my earnest desire, that in this weighty matter, we may be so truly humbled as to be favored with a clear understanding of the mind of Truth, and follow it; this would be of more advantage to the Society than any medium not in the clearness of Divine wisdom. The case is difficult to some who have slaves: but if such set aside all self-interest, and come to be weaned from the desire of getting estates, or even from holding them together, when Truth requires the contrary, I believe way will open that they will know how to steer through those difficulties."

Many Friends appeared to be deeply bowed under the weight of the work; and manifested much firmness in their love to the cause of Truth and universal righteousness on the earth. Though none openly justified the practice of slave-keeping in general, yet some appeared concerned, lest the meeting should go into such measures as might give uneasiness to many brethren; alleging that if Friends patiently continued under the exercise, the Lord, in time to come, might open a way for the deliverance of these people. Finding an engagement to speak, I said, "My mind is often led to consider the purity of the Divine Being, and the justice of his judgments; and herein my soul is covered with awfulness. I cannot omit to hint of some cases, where people have not been treated with the purity of justice, and the event hath been lamentable. Many slaves on this continent are oppressed, and their cries have reached the ears of the Most High. Such are the purity and certainty of his judgments, that he cannot be partial in our favor. In infinite love and goodness, he hath opened our understandings from one time to another, concerning our duty toward this people, and it is not a time for delay. Should we now be sensible of what he requires of us, and through a respect to the private interest of some persons, or through a regard to some friendships which do not stand on an immutable foundation, neglect to do our duty in firmness and constancy, still waiting for some extraordinary means to bring about their deliverance, it may be that God may answer us, in this matter, by terrible things in righteousness."

Many faithful brethren labored with great firmness; and the love of Truth, in a good degree, prevailed. Several Friends who had negroes, expressed their desire that a rule might be made, to deal with such Friends as offenders who bought slaves in future. To this it was answered, that the root of this evil would never be effectually struck at, until a thorough search was made into the circumstances of such Friends who kept negroes, with respect to the righteousness of their motives in keeping them, that impartial justice might be administered throughout. Several Friends expressed their desire, that a visit might be made to such as kept slaves; and many Friends said that they believed liberty was the negroes' right; to which, at length, no opposition was made publicly. A minute was made on that subject, more full than any heretofore; and the names of several Friends entered, who were free to join in a visit to such who kept slaves.

CHAPTER VI

His visiting the Quarterly Meetings in Chester county; and afterwards joining with Daniel Stanton and John Scarborough, in a visit to such as kept slaves there — Some observations on the conduct those should maintain who are concerned to speak in meetings for discipline — Several visits to such who kept slaves: and to Friends near Salem — Some account of the Yearly Meeting in the year 1759; and of the increasing concern, in divers provinces, to labor against buying and keeping slaves — The Yearly Meeting epistle — His thoughts on the smallpox spreading — and on inoculation.

On the 11th day of the eleventh month, in the year 1758, I set out for Concord; the Quarterly Meeting heretofore held there, was now, by reason of a great increase of members, divided into two by the agreement of Friends, at our last Yearly Meeting. Here I met with our beloved friends Samuel Spavold and Mary Kirby from England, and with Joseph White from Bucks county, who had taken leave of his family in order to go on a religious visit to Friends in England; and through Divine goodness, we were favored with a strengthening opportunity together.

After this meeting I joined with my friends Daniel Stanton and John Scarborough, in visiting Friends who had slaves; and at night we had a family meeting at William Trimble's, many young people being there; and it was a precious reviving opportunity. Next morning we had a comfortable sitting with a sick neighbor; and thence to the burial of the corpse of a Friend at Uwchland meeting, at which were many people, and it was a time of Divine favor; after which, we visited some who had slaves; and at night had a family meeting at a

Friend's house, where the channel of Gospel love was opened, and my mind was comforted after a hard day's labor. The next day we were at Goshen Monthly Meeting: and thence on the 18th day of the eleventh month, in the year 1758, attended the Quarterly Meeting at London Grove, it being the first held at that place. Here we met again with all the before-mentioned Friends, and had some edifying meetings. Near the conclusion of the meeting for business, Friends were incited to constancy in supporting the testimony of Truth, and reminded of the necessity which the disciples of Christ are under to attend principally to his business, as he is pleased to open it to us; and to be particularly careful to have our minds redeemed from the love of wealth; to have our outward affairs in as little room as may be; that no temporal concerns may entangle our affections, or hinder us from diligently following the dictates of Truth, in laboring to promote the pure spirit of meekness and heavenly-mindedness amongst the children of men, in these days of calamity and distress; wherein God is visiting our land with his just judgments.

Each of these Quarterly Meetings were large, and sat nearly eight hours. Here I had occasion to consider that it is a weighty thing to speak much in large meetings for business. Except our minds are rightly prepared, and we clearly understand the case we speak to, instead of forwarding, we hinder business, and make more labor for those on whom the burden of the work is laid.

If selfish views for a partial spirit have any room in our minds, we are unfit for the Lord's work; if we have a clear prospect of the business, and proper weight on our minds to speak, it behoves us to avoid useless apologies and repetitions. Where people are gathered from afar, and adjourning a meeting of business is attended with great difficulty, it behoves all to be cautious how they detain a meeting; especially when it has sat six or seven hours, and Friends have a great distance to ride home.

In the beginning of the twelfth month of the year 1758, I joined my friends John Sykes and Daniel Stanton, in visiting such who had slaves: some whose hearts were rightly exercised about them, appeared to be glad of our visit; but in some places our way was more difficult; and I often saw the necessity of keeping down to that root from whence our concern proceeded; and have cause, in reverent thankfulness, humbly to bow down before the Lord, who was near to me, and preserved my mind in calmness under some sharp conflicts, and begat a spirit of sympathy and tenderness in me, toward some who were grievously entangled by the spirit of this world.

In the first month of the year 1759, having found my mind drawn to visit some of the more active members in our Society at Philadelphia, who had slaves, I met my friend John Churchman there by an agreement; and we continued about a week in the city. We visited some that were sick, and some widows and their families; and the other part of our time was mostly employed in visiting such who had slaves. It was a time of deep exercise, looking often to the Lord for his assistance; who, in unspeakable kindness, favored us with the influence of that spirit, which crucifies to the greatness and splendor of this world, and enabled us to go through some heavy labors, in which we found peace.

On the 24th day of the third month, of this year, I was at our general spring meeting of Philadelphia; after which I again joined with John Churchman on a visit to some Friends who had slaves, in Philadelphia; and with thankfulness to our heavenly Father, I may say that Divine love and a true sympathizing tenderness of heart, prevailed at times in this service.

Having, at times, perceived a shyness in some Friends of considerable note towards me, I found an engagement in Gospel love to pay a visit to one of them; and as I dwelt under the exercise, I felt a resignedness in my mind to go. I went and told him in private, that I had a desire to have an opportunity with him alone; to which he readily agreed: and then in the fear of the Lord, things relating to that shyness were reached to the bottom; and we had a large conference, which, I believe, was of use to both of us; and am thankful that way was opened for it.

On the 14th day of the sixth month, in the same year having felt drawings in my mind to visit Friends about Salem, and having the approbation of our Monthly Meeting therein, I attended their Quarterly Meeting, and was out seven days, and at seven meetings; in some of which I was chiefly silent, and in others, through the baptizing power of Truth, my heart was enlarged in heavenly love, and I found a near fellowship with the brethren and sisters in the manifold trials attending their Christian progress through this world.

In the seventh month, I found an increasing concern on my mind to visit some active members in our Society who had slaves; and having no opportunity of the company of such who were named on the minutes of the Yearly Meeting, I went alone to their houses, and in the fear of the Lord, acquainted them with the exercise I was under: and thus, sometimes by a few words, I found myself discharged from a heavy burden.

After this, our friend John Churchman coming into our province with a view to be at some meetings, and to join again in the visit to those who had slaves, I bore him company in the said visit to some active members, and found inward satisfaction.

At our Yearly Meeting in the year 1759, we had some weighty seasons, where the power of Truth was largely extended, to the strengthening of the honest-minded. As Friends read over the epistles to be sent to the Yearly Meetings on this continent, I observed in most of them, both this year and last, that it was recommended to Friends to labor against buying and keeping slaves; and in some of them closely treated upon. As this practice hath long been a heavy exercise to me, and I have often waded through mortifying labors on that account, and at times, in some meetings, been almost alone therein, observing now the increasing concern in our religious Society, and seeing how the Lord was raising up and qualifying servants for his work, not only in this respect, but for promoting the cause of Truth in general, I was humbly bowed in thankfulness before him. This meeting continued nearly a week; and for several days, in the fore part of it, my mind was drawn into a deep inward stillness; and being at times covered with the spirit of supplication, my heart was secretly poured out before the Lord. Near the conclusion of the meeting for business way opened, that in the pure flowings of Divine love, I expressed what lay upon me; which, as it then arose in my mind, was "first to show how deep answers to deep in the hearts of the sincere and upright; though in their different growths they may not all have attained to the same clearness in some points relating to our testimony. I was led to mention the integrity and constancy of many martyrs, who gave their lives for the testimony of Jesus; and yet, in some points, held doctrines distinguishable from some which we hold; and that in all ages where people were faithful to the light and understanding which the Most High afforded them, they found acceptance with him; and that now, though there are different ways of thinking amongst us in some particulars, yet, if we mutually kept to that spirit and power which crucifies to the world, which teaches us to be content with things really needful, and to avoid all superfluities, giving up our hearts to fear and serve the Lord, true unity may still be preserved amongst us. If such who were at times under sufferings on account of some scruples of conscience, kept low and humble, and in their conduct in life manifested a spirit of true charity, it would be more likely to reach the witness in others, and be of more service in the church, than if their sufferings were attended with a contrary spirit and conduct." In this exercise I was drawn into a sympathizing tenderness with the sheep of Christ, however distinguished one from another in this world; and the like disposition appeared to spread over others in the meeting. Great is the goodness of the Lord toward his poor creatures.

An epistle went forth from this Yearly Meeting, which I think good to give a place in this journal; being as follows:—

"From the Yearly Meeting held at Philadelphia, for Pennsylvania and New Jersey, from the 22d day of the ninth month, to the 28th day of the same, inclusive, 1759.

"*To the Quarterly and Monthly Meetings of Friends belonging to the said Yearly Meeting.*

"Dearly beloved friends and brethren.

"IN an awful sense of the wisdom and goodness of the Lord our God, whose tender mercies have long been continued to us in this land, we affectionately salute you, with sincere and fervent desires, that we may reverently regard the dispensations of his providence, and improve under them.

"The empires and kingdoms of the earth are subject to his Almighty power. He is the God of the spirits of all flesh; and deals with his people agreeably to that wisdom, the depth whereof is to us unsearchable. We in these provinces, may say he hath, as a gracious and tender Parent, dealt bountifully with us, even from the days of our fathers. It was he who strengthened them to labor through the difficulties attending the improvement of a wilderness, and made way for them in the hearts of the natives; so that by them they were comforted in times of want and distress. It was by the gracious influences of his holy Spirit, that they were disposed to work righteousness, and walk uprightly one towards another, and towards the natives, and in life and conversation to manifest the excellency of principles and doctrines of the Christian religion; and thereby they retain their esteem and friendship. Whilst they were laboring for the necessaries of life, many of them were fervently engaged to promote piety and virtue in the earth, and to educate their children in the fear of the Lord.

"If we carefully consider the peaceable measures pursued in the first settlement of the land, and that freedom from the desolations of wars, which for a long time we enjoyed, we shall find ourselves under strong obligations to the Almighty, who, when the earth is so generally polluted with wickedness, gave us a being in a part so signally favored with tranquillity and plenty, and in which the glad tidings of the Gospel of Christ are so freely published, that we may justly say with the psalmist, 'What shall we render unto the Lord for all his benefits?'

"Our own real good, and the good of our posterity in some measure depend on the part we act; and it nearly concerns us to try our foundations impartially. Such are the different rewards of the just and unjust in a future state, that to attend diligently to the dictates of the spirit of Christ, to devote ourselves to his service and engage fervently in his cause, during our short stay in this world, is a choice well becoming a free intelligent creature. We shall thus clearly see and consider that the dealings of God with mankind in a national capacity, as recorded in holy writ, sufficiently evidence the truth of that saying, 'it is righteousness which exalteth a nation'; and though he doth not at all times suddenly execute his judgments on a sinful people in this life, yet we see by many instances, that where 'men follow lying vanities, they forsake their own mercies.' As a proud selfish spirit prevails and spreads among a people, so partial judgment, oppression, discord, envy, and confusion increase, and provinces and kingdoms are made to drink the cup of adversity as a reward of their own doings. Thus the inspired prophet, reasoning with the degenerated Jews, saith, 'Thine own wickedness shall correct thee, and thy backslidings shall reprove thee: know, therefore, that it is an evil thing and bitter, that thou hast forsaken the Lord thy God, and that my fear is not in thee, saith the Lord God of hosts.'

"The God of our fathers, who hath bestowed on us many benefits, furnished a table for us in the wilderness, and made the deserts and solitary places to rejoice, doth now mercifully call upon us to serve him more faithfully. We may truly say with the prophet, 'it is his voice which crieth to the city, and men of wisdom see his name: They regard the rod, and him who hath appointed it.'—People who look chiefly at things outward, too little consider the original cause of the present troubles; but such who fear the Lord, and think often upon his name, they see and feel that a wrong spirit is spreading among the inhabitants of our country; that the hearts of many are waxed fat, and their ears dull of hearing; that the Most High, in his visitations to us, instead of calling, lifteth up his voice and crieth; he crieth to our country, and his voice waxeth louder and louder. In former wars between the English and other nations, since the settlement of our provinces, the calamities attending them that have fallen chiefly on other places, but of late they have reached our borders. Many of our fellow-subjects have suffered on and near our frontiers, some have been slain in battle, some killed in their houses, and some in their fields; some wounded and left in great misery, and others separated from their wives and little children, who have been carried captives among the Indians. We have seen men and women, who have been witnesses of these scenes of sorrow, and being reduced to want, have come to our houses asking relief. It is not long since it was the case of many young men in one of these provinces to be drafted, in order to be taken as soldiers. Some were at that time in great distress, and had occasion to consider that their lives had been too little conformable to the purity and spirituality of that religion which we profess, and found themselves too little acquainted with that inward humility, in which true fortitude to endure hardness for the Truth's sake is experienced. Many parents were concerned for their children, and in that time of trial were led to consider, that their care to get outward treasure for them, had been greater than their care for their settlement in that religion which crucifieth to the world, and enableth to bear a clear testimony to the peaceable government of the Messiah. These troubles are removed, and for a time we are released from them.

"Let us not forget that 'the Most High hath his way in the deep, in clouds and in thick darkness'—that it is his voice which crieth to the city and to the country; and oh! that these loud and awakening cries may have a proper effect upon us, that heavier chastisement may not become necessary! For though things, as to the outward, may for a short time afford a pleasing prospect, yet while a selfish spirit, that is not subject to the cross of Christ, continueth to spread and prevail, there can be no long continuance in outward peace and tranquillity. If we desire an inheritance incorruptible, and to be at rest in that state of peace and happiness, which ever continues; if we desire in this life to dwell under the favor and protection of that Almighty Being, whose habitation is in holiness, whose ways are all equal and whose anger is now kindled, because of our backslidings; let us then awfully regard these beginnings of his sore judgments, and with abasement and humiliation turn to him whom we have offended.

"Contending with one equal in strength, is an uneasy exercise; but if the Lord becomes our enemy, if we persist to contend with him who is omnipotent, our overthrow will be unavoidable.

"Do we feel an affectionate regard to posterity; and are we employed to promote their happiness? Do our minds, in things outward, look beyond our own dissolution; and are we contriving for the prosperity of our children after us? Let us then, like wise builders, lay the foundation deep; and by our constant uniform regard to inward piety and virtue, let them see that we really value it. Let us labor in the fear of the Lord, that their innocent minds, while young and tender, may be preserved from corruption; that as they advance in age, they may rightly understand their true interests, may consider the uncertainty of temporal things, and above all, have their hope and confidence firmly settled in the blessing of that Almighty Being who inhabits eternity, and preserves and supports the world.

"In all our cares about worldly treasures, let us steadily bear in mind, that riches possessed by children who do not truly serve God, are likely to prove snares that may grievously entangle them in that spirit of selfishness and exaltation, which stands in opposition to real peace and happiness; and renders those enemies to the cross of Christ, who submit to the influence of it.

"To keep a watchful eye towards real objects of charity, to visit the poor in their lonesome dwelling-places, to comfort those who, through the dispensations of Divine Providence, are in strait and painful circumstances in this life, and steadily to endeavor to honor God with our substance, from a real sense of the love of Christ influencing our minds thereto, is more likely to bring a blessing to our children, and will afford more satisfaction to a Christian favored with plenty, than an earnest desire to collect much wealth to leave behind us; for 'here we have no continuing city'; may we therefore diligently 'seek one that is to come, whose builder and maker is God.'

"'Finally, brethren, whatsoever things are true, whatsoever things are just, whatsoever things are lovely, whatsoever things are of good report; if there be any virtue, if there be any praise, think on these things and do them, and the God of peace shall be with you.'

"Signed by appointment, and on behalf of our said meeting, by seven Friends."

On the 28th day of the eleventh month, in the year 1759, I was at the Quarterly Meeting in Bucks county. This day being the meeting of ministers and elders, my heart was enlarged in the love of Jesus Christ; and the favor of the most High was extended to us in that and the ensuing meeting.

I had conversation at my lodging, with my beloved friend Samuel Eastburn; who expressed a concern to join in a visit to some Friends in that country who had negroes; and as I had felt a draught in my mind to that work in the said country, I came home and put things in order. On the 11th day of the twelfth month following, I went over the river; and on the next day was at Buckingham meeting; where, through the descendings of heavenly dew, my mind was comforted and drawn into near unity with the flock of Jesus Christ.

Entering upon this visit appeared weighty; and before I left home my mind was often sad; under which exercise I felt, at times, the Holy Spirit which helps our infirmities; through which, in private, my prayers were at times put up to God, that he would please to purge me from all selfishness, that I might be strengthened to discharge my duty faithfully, how hard soever to the natural part. We proceeded on the visit in a weighty frame of spirit, and went to the houses of the most active members throughout the country who had negroes; and through the goodness of the Lord, my mind was preserved in resignation in times of trial, and though the work was hard to nature, yet through the strength of that love which is stronger than death, tenderness of heart was often felt amongst us in our visits, and we parted from several families with greater satisfaction than we expected.

We visited Joseph White's family, he being in England; had also a family sitting at the house of an elder who bore us company, and was at Makefield on a first-day; at all which times my heart was truly thankful to the Lord, who was graciously pleased to renew his loving kindness to us, his poor servants, uniting us together in his work.

In the winter of this year, the smallpox being in our town, and many being inoculated, of which a few died, some things were opened in my mind, which I wrote as follows:—

The more fully our lives are conformable to the will of God, the better it is for us. I have looked on the smallpox as a messenger from the Almighty, to be an assistant in the cause of virtue, and to incite us to consider whether we employ our time in such things only as are consistent with perfect wisdom and goodness.

Building houses suitable to dwell in, for ourselves and our creatures; preparing clothing suitable for the climate and season, and food convenient, are duties incumbent on us: and under these general heads are many branches of business, in which we may venture health and life, as necessity may require.

This disease being in a house, and my business calling me to go near it, it incites me to think, whether this business is a real indispensable duty; whether it is not in conformity to some custom which would be better laid aside; or whether it does not proceed from too eager a pursuit after outward treasure. If the business before me springs not from a clear understanding, and a regard to that use of things which perfect wisdom approves; to be brought to a sense of it, and stopped in my pursuit, is a kindness; for when I proceed to business without some evidence of duty, I have found by experience that it tends to weakness.

If I am so situated that there appears no probability of missing the infection, it tends to make me think, whether my manner of life in things outward, has nothing in it which may unfit my body to receive this messenger, in a way the most favorable to me. Do I use food and drink in no other sort, and in no other degree, than was designed by Him who gave these creatures for our sustenance? Do I never abuse my body by inordinate labor, striving to accomplish some end which I have unwisely proposed? Do I use action enough in some useful employ? Or do I sit too much idle, while some persons who labor to support me have too great a share of it? If in any of these things I am deficient, to be incited to consider it, is a favor to me.

Employment is necessary in social life; and this infection which often proves mortal, incites me to think, whether these social acts of mine are real duties: if I go on a visit to the widows and fatherless, do I go purely on a principle of charity, free from any selfish views? If I go to a religious meeting, it puts me on thinking, whether I go in sincerity and a clear sense of duty; or whether it is not partly in conformity to custom, or partly from a sensible delight which my animal spirits feel in the company of other people; and whether to support my reputation as a religious man, has no share in it.

Do affairs relating to civil society call me near this infection? If I go, it is at the hazard of my health and life; and it becomes me to think seriously, whether love to Truth and righteousness is the motive of my attending; whether the manner of proceeding is altogether equitable; or whether aught of narrowness, party interest, respect to outward dignities, names or distinctions among men, stains the beauty of those assemblies, and renders it doubtful in point of duty, whether a disciple of Christ ought to attend as a member united to the body or not.

Whenever there are blemishes which remain for a series of time, that which is a means of stirring us up to look attentively on these blemishes, and to labor according to our capacities, to have health and soundness restored in our country, we may justly account a kindness from our gracious Father, who appointed that mean.

The care of a wise and good man for his only son, is inferior to the regard of the great Parent of the universe for his creatures. He hath the command of all the powers and operations in nature; and "doth not afflict willingly, nor grieve the children of men": chastisement is intended for instruction, and instruction being received by gentle chastisement, greater calamities are prevented.

By an earthquake, hundreds of houses are sometimes shaken down in a few minutes, and multitudes of people perish suddenly; and many more being crushed and bruised in the ruins of the buildings, pine away and die in great misery.

By the breaking in of enraged, merciless armies, flourishing countries have been laid waste, great numbers of people have perished in a short time, and many more been pressed with poverty and grief.

By the pestilence, people have died so fast in a city, that through fear, grief, and confusion, those in health have found great difficulty in burying the dead, even without coffins.

By famine, great numbers of people, in some places, have been brought to the utmost distress, and pined away for want of the necessaries of life. Thus, where the kind invitations and gentle chastisements of a gracious God have not been attended to, his sore judgments have, at times, been poured out upon people.

While some rules approved in civil society, and conformable to human policy, so called, are distinguishable from the purity of Truth and righteousness; while many, professing Truth, are declining from that ardent love and heavenly-mindedness, which were amongst the primitive followers of Jesus Christ, it is a time for us to attend diligently to the intent of every chastisement, and consider the most deep and inward design of them.

The Most High doth not often speak with an outward voice to our outward ears; but if we humbly meditate on his perfections, consider that He is perfect wisdom and goodness, and that to afflict his creatures to no purpose, would be utterly averse to his nature, we shall hear and understand his language, both in his gentle and more heavy chastisements; and take heed that we do not, in the wisdom of this world, endeavor to escape his hand by means too powerful for us.

Had he endowed men with understanding to hinder the force of this disease by innocent means, which had never proved mortal nor hurtful to our bodies, such discovery might be considered as the period of chastisement by this distemper, where that knowledge extended.° But as life and health are his gifts, and not to be disposed of in our own wills, to take upon us, when in health, a distemper of which some die, requires great clearness of knowledge, that it is our duty to do so.

CHAPTER VII

His visit in company with Samuel Eastburn, to Long Island, Rhode Island, Boston, etc., in New England — Remarks on the slave trade at Newport, and his exercise on that account; also on lotteries — Some observations on the island of Nantucket.

HAVING for some time past felt a sympathy in my mind with Friends eastward, I opened my concern in our Monthly Meeting; and obtaining a certificate, set forward on the 17th day of the fourth month, in the year 1760, joining in company, by a previous agreement, with my beloved friend Samuel Eastburn. We had meetings at Woodbridge, Rahway, and Plainfield; and were at their Monthly Meeting of ministers and elders in Rahway. We labored under some discouragement; but through the invisible power of Truth, our visit was made reviving to the lowly-minded, with whom I felt a near unity of spirit, being much reduced in my mind. We passed on and visited most of the meetings on Long Island. It was my concern from day to day, to say no more nor less than what the Spirit of Truth opened in me, being jealous over myself lest I should speak anything to make my testimony look agreeable to that mind in people, which is not in pure obedience to the cross of Christ.

The spring of the ministry was often low; and through the subjecting power of Truth, we were kept low with it; and from place to place, such whose hearts were truly concerned for the cause of Christ, appeared to be comforted in our labors; and though it was in general a time of abasement of the creature, yet through His goodness, who is a helper of the poor, we had some poor edifying seasons both in meetings and in families where we tarried; and sometimes found strength to labor earnestly with the unfaithful, especially with those whose station in families, or in the Society was such, that their example had a powerful tendency to open the way for others to go aside from the purity and soundness of the blessed Truth. At Jericho, on Long Island, I wrote home as follows: —

"24th of the Fourth month, 1760.

"Dearly beloved wife,

"WE are favored with health; have been at sundry meetings in East Jersey, and on this island: my mind hath been much in an inward watchful frame since I left thee, greatly desiring that our proceedings may be singly in the will of our heavenly Father.

"As the present appearance of things is not joyous, I have been much shut up from outward cheerfulness, remembering that promise, 'Then shalt thou delight thyself in the Lord.' As this, from day to day, has been revived in my memory, I have considered that his internal presence on our minds, is a delight of all others the most pure; and that the honest-hearted not only delight in this, but in the effect of it upon them. He who regards the helpless and distressed, reveals his love to his children under affliction, and they delight in beholding his benevolence, and feeling Divine charity moving upon them. Of this I may speak a little; for though, since I left you, I have often found an engaging love and affection toward thee and my daughter, and friends about home, that going out at this time, when sickness is so great amongst you, is a trial upon me; yet I often remember there are many widows and fatherless, many who have poor tutors, many who have evil examples before them, and many whose minds are in captivity; for whose sake my heart is at times moved with compassion, that I feel my mind resigned to leave you for a season, to exercise that gift which the Lord hath bestowed on me; which, though small, compared with some, yet in this I rejoice, that I feel love unfeigned toward my fellow-creatures. I recommend you to the Almighty, who, I trust, cares for you; and under a sense of his heavenly love remain "Thy loving husband,

"J. W."

We crossed from the east end of Long Island to New London, about thirty miles, in a large open boat; while we were out, the wind rising high, the waves several times beat over us, and to me it appeared dangerous; but my mind was at that time, turned to Him who made and governs the deep, and my life was resigned to him: and as he was mercifully pleased to preserve us, I had fresh occasion to consider every day as a day lent to me; and felt a renewed engagement to devote my time and all I had to Him who gave it.

We had five meetings in Narraganset; and went thence to Newport on Rhode Island. Our gracious Father preserved us in an humble dependence on him through deep exercises, that were mortifying to the creaturely will. In several families in the country where we lodged, I felt an engagement on my mind to have a conference with them in private concerning their slaves; and through Divine aid, I was favored to give up thereto. Though, in this concern, I appear singular from many whose service in travelling I believe is greater than mine, I do not think hard of them for omitting it; nor do I repine at having so unpleasant a task assigned me, but look with awfulness to Him, who appoints to his servants their respective employments, and is good to all who serve him sincerely.

We got to Newport in the evening, and on the next day visited two sick persons, and had comfortable sittings with them; and in the afternoon attended the burial of a Friend.

The next day we were at meetings at Newport, in the forenoon and afternoon; where the spring of the ministry was opened, and strength given to declare the word of life to the people.

The next day we went on our journey; but the great number of slaves in these parts, and the continuance of that trade from thence to Guinea, made a deep impression on me; and my cries were often put up to my heavenly Father in secret, that he would enable me to discharge my duty faithfully, in such way as he might be pleased to point out to me.

We took Swansea, Freetown, and Taunton, in our way to Boston; where also we had a meeting; our exercise was deep, and the love of Truth prevailed, for which I bless the Lord. We went eastward about eighty miles beyond Boston, taking meetings, and were in a good degree preserved in an humble dependence on that arm which drew us out; and though we had some hard labor with the disobedient, laying things closely home to such as were stout against the Truth; yet through the goodness of God, we had at times to partake of heavenly comfort with them who were meek, and were often favored to part with Friends in the nearness of true Gospel fellowship. We returned to Boston, and had another comfortable opportunity with Friends there; and thence rode back a day's journey eastward of Boston. — Our guide being a heavy man, and the weather hot, and my companion and I considering it, expressed our freedom to go on without him, to which he consented, and we respectfully took our leave of him; we did this, believing the journey would be hard to him and his horse.

We visited the meetings in those parts, and were measurably baptized into a feeling of the state of the Society; and in bowedness of spirit went to the Yearly Meeting at Newport; where I understood that a large number of slaves had been imported from Africa into that town, and were then on sale by a member of our Society. At this meeting we met with John Storer from England, Elizabeth Shipley, Ann Gaunt, Hannah Foster, and Mercy Redman from our parts, all ministers of the Gospel, of whose company I was glad.

At this time my appetite failed, and I grew outwardly weak,

and had a feeling of the condition of Habakkuk, as thus expressed: "When I heard my belly trembled, my lips quivered, I trembled in myself that I might rest in the day of trouble." I had many cogitations, and was sorely distressed; and was desirous that Friends might petition the legislature, to use their endeavors to discourage the future importation of slaves; for I saw that this trade was a great evil, and tended to multiply troubles and bring distresses on the people in those parts, for whose welfare my heart was deeply concerned.

But I perceived several difficulties in regard to petitioning; and such was the exercise of my mind, that I thought of endeavoring to get an opportunity to speak a few words in the House of Assembly, then sitting in town. This exercise came upon me in the afternoon, on the second day of the Yearly Meeting, and going to bed, I got no sleep till my mind was wholly resigned therein; and in the morning I inquired of a Friend how long the Assembly were likely to continue sitting; who told me, they were expected to be prorogued that day or the next.

As I was desirous to attend the business of the meeting, and perceived that the Assembly were likely to depart before the business was over, after considerable exercise, humbly seeking to the Lord for instruction, my mind settled to attend on the business of the meeting. I had prepared a short essay of a petition to be presented to the legislature, if way opened; and being informed that there were some appointed by that Yearly Meeting, to speak with those in authority, in cases relating to the Society, I opened my mind to several of them, and showed them the essay I had made; and afterward opened the case in the meeting for business, in substance as follows: —

"I have been under a concern for some time, on account of the great number of slaves who are imported into this colony. I am aware that it is a tender point to speak to, but apprehend I am not clear in the sight of heaven without speaking to it. I have prepared an essay of a petition, if way open, to be presented to the legislature; and what I have to propose to this meeting is, that some Friends may be named to withdraw and look over it, and report whether they believe it suitable to be read in the meeting; if they should think well of reading it, it will remain for the meeting, after hearing it, to consider whether to take any further notice of it as a meeting or not." After a short conference some Friends went out, and looking over it, expressed their willingness to have it read; which being done, many expressed their unity with the proposal; and some signified, that to have the subjects of the petition enlarged upon, and to be signed out of meeting by such who were free, would be more suitable than to do it there. Though I expected at first, that if it was done it would be in that way, yet such was the exercise of my mind, that to move it in the hearing of Friends when assembled, appeared to me a duty. My heart yearned toward the inhabitants of these parts, believing that by this trade there had been an increase of inquietude amongst them, and a way made easy for the spreading of a spirit opposite to that meekness and humility which is a sure resting-place for the soul; and that the continuance of this trade would not only render their healing more difficult, but increase their malady.

Having proceeded thus far, I felt easy to leave the essay amongst Friends, for them to dispose of as they believed best. And now an exercise revived on my mind in relation to lotteries, which were common in those parts. I had moved it in a former sitting of this meeting, when arguments were used in favor of Friends being held excused, who were only concerned in such lotteries as were agreeable to law. On moving it again, it was opposed as before; but the hearts of some solid Friends appeared to be united to discourage the practice amongst their members; and the matter was zealously handled by some on both sides. In this debate it appeared very clear to me, that the spirit of lotteries was a spirit of selfishness, which tended to confusion and darkness of understanding; and that pleading for it in our meetings, set apart for the Lord's work, was not right: and in the heat of zeal, I once made reply to what an ancient Friend said, and when I sat down, I saw that my words were not enough seasoned with charity; and after this I spoke no more on the subject. At length a minute was made; a copy of which was agreed to be sent to their several Quarterly Meetings, inciting Friends to labor to discourage the practice amongst all professing with us.

Some time after this minute was made, I remaining uneasy with the manner of my speaking to the ancient Friend, could not see my way clear to conceal my uneasiness, but was concerned that I might say nothing to weaken the cause in which I had labored. After some close exercise and hearty repentance that I had not attended closely to the safe guide, I stood up, and reciting the passage, acquainted Friends that though I dare not go from what I had said as to the matter, yet I was uneasy with the manner of my speaking, believing milder language would have been better. As this was uttered in some degree of creaturely abasement, it appeared to have a good savor amongst us, after a warm debate.

The Yearly Meeting being now over, there remained on my mind a secret, though heavy exercise in regard to some leading active members about Newport, being in the practice of slave-keeping. This I mentioned to two ancient Friends who came out of the country, and proposed to them, if way opened, to have some conversation with those Friends: and thereupon, one of those country Friends and I consulted one of the most noted elders who had slaves; and he, in a respectful manner, encouraged me to proceed to clear myself of what lay upon me. I had had, near the beginning of the Yearly Meeting, a private conference with this elder and his wife, concerning theirs; so that the way seemed clear to me, to advise with him about the manner of proceeding. I told him, I was free to have a conference with them all together in a private house; or if he thought they would take it unkind to be asked to come together, and to be spoken with in the hearing of each other, I was free to spend some time among them, and visit them all in their own houses. He expressed his liking to the first proposal, not doubting their willingness to come together; and as I proposed a visit to ministers, elders, and overseers only, he named some others, whom he desired might be present also. As a careful messenger was wanted to acquaint them in a proper manner, he offered to go to all their houses to open the matter to them; and did so. — About the eighth hour next morning, we met in the meeting-house chamber, and the last-mentioned country Friend, also my companion and John Storer, with us; when, after a short time of retirement, I acquainted them with the steps I had taken in procuring that meeting, opened the concern I was under, and we proceeded to a free conference upon the subject. My exercise was heavy, and I was deeply bowed in spirit before the Lord, who was pleased to favor with the seasoning virtue of Truth, which wrought a tenderness amongst us; and the subject was mutually handled in a calm and peaceful spirit. At length feeling my mind released from the burthen which I had been under, I took my leave of them in a good degree of satisfaction; and by the tenderness they manifested in regard to the practice, and the concern several of them expressed in relation to the manner of disposing of their negroes after their decease, I believed that a good exercise was spreading amongst them; and I am humbly thankful to God, who supported my mind, and preserved me in a good degree of resignation through these trials.

Thou, who sometimes travels in the work of the ministry, and art made very welcome by thy friends, and seest many tokens of their satisfaction, in having thee for their guest; it is good for thee to dwell deep, that thou mayest feel and understand the spirits of people. If we believe Truth points towards a conference on some subjects, in a private way, it is needful for us to take heed that their kindness, their freedom, and affability, do not hinder us from the Lord's word. I have seen, that in the midst of kindness and smooth conduct, to speak close and home to them who entertain us, on points that relate to their outward interest, is hard labor; and sometimes when I have felt Truth lead toward it, I have found myself disqualified by a superficial friendship. As the sense thereof hath abased me, and my cries have been to the Lord, I have been humbled and made content to appear weak, or as a fool for his sake; and thus a door hath opened to enter upon it. To attempt to do the Lord's work in our own way, and to speak of that which is the burthen of the word, in a way easy to the natural part, doth not reach the bottom of the disorder. To see the failings of our friends, and think hard of them, without opening that which we ought to open, and still carry a face of friendship, this tends to undermine the foundation of true unity.

The office of a minister of Christ is weighty; and they who now go forth as watchmen, had need to be steadily on their guard against the snares of prosperity and an outside friendship.

After the Yearly Meeting we were at meetings at Newtown, Acushnet, Cushnet, Long Plain, Rochester, and Dartmouth. From thence we sailed for Nantucket, in company with Ann Gaunt and Mercy Redman, and several other Friends: the wind being slack, we only reached Tarpawling Cove the first day; where, going on shore, we found room in a public house, and beds for a few of us, the rest sleeping on the floor. We went on board again about break of day; and though the wind was small, we were favored to come within about four miles of Nantucket; and about ten of us getting into our boat, we rowed to the harbor before dark; whereupon a large boat going off, brought in the rest of the passengers about midnight. The next day but one was their Yearly Meeting, which held four days; the last of which was the Monthly Meeting for business. We had a laborious time amongst them; our minds were closely exercised, and I believe it was a time of great searching of heart: the longer I was on the island, the more I became sensible that there was a considerable number of valuable Friends there, though an evil spirit, tending to strife, had been at work amongst them. I was cautious of making any visits, but as my mind was particularly drawn to them; and in that way we had some sittings in Friends' houses, where the heavenly wing was at times spread over us, to our mutual comfort.

My beloved companion had very acceptable service on this island.

When meeting was over, we all agreed to sail the next day, if the weather was suitable and we well; and being called up the latter part of the night, we went on board a vessel, being in all about fifty; but the wind changing, the seamen thought best to stay in the harbor till it altered; so we returned on shore. Feeling clear as to any further visits, I spent my time in our chamber chiefly alone; and after some hours, my heart being filled with the spirit of supplication, my prayers and tears were poured out before my heavenly Father, for his help and instruction in the manifold difficulties which attended me in life. While I was waiting upon the Lord, there came a messenger from the women Friends, who lodged at another house, desiring to confer with us about appointing a meeting, which to me appeared weighty, as we had been at so many before; but after a short conference, and advising with some elderly Friends, a meeting was appointed, in which the Friend who first moved it, and who had been much shut up before, was largely opened in the love of the Gospel. The next morning about break of day, going again on board the vessel, we reached Falmouth on the main before night; where our horses being brought, we proceeded toward Sandwich Quarterly Meeting.

Being two days in going to Nantucket, and having been there

once before, I observed many shoals in their bay, which make sailing more dangerous, especially in stormy nights; also, that a great shoal, which encloses their harbor, prevents their going in with sloops, except when the tide is up. Waiting without this shoal for the rising of the tide, is sometimes hazardous in storms: waiting within, they sometimes miss a fair wind. I took notice that on this small island was a great number of inhabitants, and the soil not very fertile; the timber so gone, that for vessels, fences, and firewood, they depend chiefly on the buying from the main; to answer the cost whereof, with most of their other expenses, they depend principally upon the whale fishery. I considered that as towns grew larger, and lands near navigable waters were more cleared, it would require more labor to get timber and wood. I understood that the whales being much hunted, and sometimes wounded and not killed, grew more shy and difficult to come at: I considered that the formation of the earth, the seas, the islands, bays, and rivers, the motion of the winds and great waters, which cause bars and shoals in particular places, were all the works of Him who is perfect wisdom and goodness; and as people attend to his heavenly instruction, and put their trust in him, he provides for them in all parts, where he gives them a being. In this visit to these people, I feel a strong desire for their firm establishment on the sure foundation; and besides what was said more publicly, I was concerned to speak with the women Friends, in their Monthly Meeting of business, many being present; and in the fresh spring of pure love, to open before them the advantage, both inward and outward, of attending singly to the pure guidance of the Holy Spirit, and therein to educate their children in true humility, and the disuse of all superfluities, reminding them of the difficulties their husbands and sons were frequently exposed to at sea; and that the more plain and simple their way of living was, the less need there would be of running great hazards to support them in it. I encouraged the young women in their neat decent way of attending themselves on the affairs of the house; showing, as the way opened, that where people were truly humble, used themselves to business, and were content with a plain way of life, it had ever been attended with more true peace and calmness of mind, than they have had who, aspiring to greatness and outward show, have grasped hard for an income to support themselves in it. As I observed they had few or no slaves amongst them, I had to encourage them to be content without them; making mention of the numerous troubles and vexations, which frequently attend the minds of people, who depend on slaves to do their labor.

We attended the Quarterly Meeting at Sandwich, in company with Ann Gaunt and Mercy Redman, which was preceded by a Monthly Meeting, and in the whole held three days. We were in various ways exercised amongst them in Gospel love, according to the several gifts bestowed on us; and were at times overshadowed with the virtue of Truth, to the comfort of the sincere and the stirring up of the negligent. Here we parted with Ann and Mercy, and went to Rhode Island, taking one meeting in our way, which was a satisfactory time; and reaching Newport the evening before their Quarterly Meeting, we attended it; and after that had a meeting with our young people, separated from those of other societies. We went through much labor in this town; and now in taking leave of it, though I felt close inward exercise to the last, I found peace; and was in some degree comforted in a belief that a good number remain in that place, who retain a sense of Truth; and that there are some young people attentive to the voice of the heavenly Shepherd. The last meeting in which Friends from the several parts of the quarter came together, was select; and through the renewed manifestation of the Father's love, the hearts of the sincere were united together.

That poverty of spirit and inward weakness, with which I was much tried during the fore part of this journey, has of late appeared to me to be a dispensation of kindness. Appointing meetings never appeared more weighty to me. I was led into deep search, whether in all things my mind was resigned to the will of God; often querying with myself, what should be the cause of such inward poverty; and greatly desired that no secret reserve in my heart might hinder my access to the Divine fountain. In these humbling times I was made watchful, and excited to attend to the secret movings of the heavenly principle in my mind which prepared the way to some duties, that in more easy and prosperous times as to the outward, I believe I should have been in danger of omitting.

From Newport we went to Greenwich, Shanticut, and Warwick; and were helped to labor amongst Friends in the love of our gracious Redeemer; and then, accompanied by our friend John Casey from Newport, we rode through Connecticut to Oblong, visited the meetings of Friends in those parts, and thence proceeded to the Quarterly Meeting at Ryewoods; and through the gracious extendings of Divine help, had some seasoning opportunities in those places. We visited Friends at New York and Flushing; and thence to Rahway; and here our roads parting, I took leave of my beloved companion and true yoke-mate Samuel Eastburn; and reached home on the 10th day of the eighth month, 1760, where I found my family well: and for the favors and protection of the Lord, both inward and outward, extended to me in this journey, my heart is humbled in grateful ackowledgements; and I find renewed desires to dwell and walk in resignedness before him.

CHAPTER VIII

His visits to Pennsylvania, Shrewsbury, and Squan — Publishes the second part of his Considerations on keeping negroes — The grounds of his appearing in some respects singular in his dress — Visits the families of Friends of Ancocas and Mount Holly meetings — Visits to the Indians at Wehaloosing on the river Susquehanna.

Having felt my mind drawn toward a visit to a few meetings in Pennsylvania, I was very desirous to be rightly instructed as to the time of setting off. On the 10th day of the fifth month, 1761, being the first-day of the week, I went to Haddonfield meeting, concluding to seek for heavenly instruction, and to come home or go on, as I might then believe best for me; and there, through the springing up of pure love, I felt encouragement, and so crossed the river. In this visit I was at two Quarterly and three Monthly Meetings; and in the love of Truth, felt my way open to labor with some noted Friends who kept negroes; and as I was favored to keep to the root, and endeavored to discharge what I believed was required of me, I found inward peace therein from time to time; and thankfulness of heart to the Lord, who was graciously pleased to be a guide to me.

In the eighth month, 1761, having felt drawings in my mind to visit Friends in and about Shrewsbury, I went there, and was at their Monthly Meeting, and the meeting on first-day; had a meeting at Squan, and another at Squankum; and as way opened, had conversation with some noted Friends concerning their slaves: and I returned home in a thankful sense of the goodness of the Lord.

From the care I had felt growing in me for some years, I wrote Considerations on keeping Negroes; part the second; which was printed this year 1762. When the overseers of the press had done with it, they offered to get a number printed, to be paid for out of the Yearly Meeting stock, and to be given away; but I being most easy to publish them at my own expense, and offering my reasons they appeared satisfied.

This stock is the contribution of the members of our religious Society in general; amongst whom are some who keep negroes, and being inclined to continue them in slavery, are not likely to be satisfied with those books being spread amongst a people where many of the slaves are taught to read, and especially at their expense; and such receiving them as a gift, often conceal them. But as they who make a purchase, generally buy that which they have a mind for, I believed it best to sell them; expecting, by that means, they would more generally be read with attention. Advertisements being signed by order of the overseers of the press, directed to be read in Monthly Meetings of business within our own Yearly Meeting, informing where the books were, and that the price was no more than the cost of printing and binding them; many were taken off in our parts; some I sent to Virginia, some to New York, and some to Newport, to my acquaintance there; and some I kept, expecting to give part of them away, where there appeared a prospect of service.

In my youth I was used to hard labor; and though I was middling healthy, yet my nature was not fitted to endure so much as many others. Being often weary, I was prepared to sympathize with those whose circumstances in life, as free men, required constant labor to answer the demands of their creditors; and with others under oppression. In the uneasiness of body, which I have many times felt by too much labor, not as a forced but a voluntary oppression, I have often been excited to think on the original cause of that oppression which is imposed on many in the world: and the latter part of the time wherein I labored on our plantation, my heart through the fresh visitations of heavenly love, being often tender; and my leisure time frequently spent in reading the life and doctrines of our blessed Redeemer, the account of the sufferings of martyrs, and the history of the first rise of our Society; a belief was gradually settled in my mind, that if such who have great estates, generally lived in that humility and plainness which belongs to a Christian life; and laid much easier rents and interests on their lands and moneys, and thus led the way to a right use of things, so great a number of people might be employed in things useful, that labor both for men and other creatures would need to be no more than an agreeable employ; and divers branches of business which serve chiefly to please the natural inclinations of our minds, and which, at present, seem necessary to circulate that wealth which some gather, might in this way of pure wisdom be discontinued. As I have thus considered these things, a query at times hath arisen; Do I in all my proceedings, keep to that use of things which is agreeable to universal righteousness? And then there hath some degree of sadness at times come over me; because I accustomed myself to some things which occasioned more labor than I believe Divine wisdom intends for us.

From an early acquaintance with Truth, I have often felt an inward distress, occasioned by the striving of a spirit in me, against the operation of the heavenly principle; and in this circumstance have been affected with a sense of my own wretchedness, and in a mourning condition felt earnest longings for that Divine help, which brings the soul into true liberty. Sometimes in this state, retiring into private places, the spirit of supplication hath been given me; and under a heavy covering, I have asked my gracious Father to give me a heart in all things resigned to the direction of his wisdom; and in uttering language like this, the thoughts of my wearing hats and garments dyed with a dye hurtful to them, have made lasting impressions on me.

In visiting people of note in the Society who had slaves, and laboring with them in brotherly love on that account, I have seen, and the sight has affected me, that a conformity to some customs distinguishable from pure wisdom, has entangled many; and that the desire of gain to support these customs, greatly opposed the work of Truth. Sometimes when the prospect of the work before me has been such, that in bowedness of spirit I have been drawn into retired places, and besought the Lord with tears that he would take me wholly under his direction, and show me the way in which I ought to walk; it has revived with strength of conviction, that if I would be his faithful servant, I must in all things attend to his wisdom, and be teachable; and cease from all customs contrary thereto, however used amongst religious people.

As he is the perfection of power, of wisdom, and of goodness, so I believe he hath provided that so much labor shall be necessary for men's support in this world, as would, being rightly divided, be a suitable employment of their time; and that we cannot go into superfluities, or grasp after wealth in a way contrary to his wisdom, without having connection with some degree of oppression, and with that spirit which leads to self-exaltation and strife, and which frequently brings calamities on countries, by parties contending about their claims.

Being thus fully convinced, and feeling an increasing desire to live in the spirit of peace; being often sorrowfully affected in thinking on the unquiet spirit in which wars are generally carried on, and with the miseries of many of my fellow-creatures engaged therein; some suddenly destroyed; some wounded, and after much pain remain cripples; some deprived of all their outward substance and reduced to want; and some carried into captivity — thinking often on these things, the use of hats and garments dyed with a dye hurtful to them, and wearing more clothes in summer than are useful, grew more uneasy to me; believing them to be customs which have not their foundation in pure wisdom. The apprehension of being singular from my beloved friends, was a strait upon me; and thus I remained in the use of some things contrary to my judgment.

On the 31st day of the fifth month, 1761, I was taken ill of a fever; and after having it near a week, I was in great distress of body. And one day there was a cry raised in me, that I might understand the cause why I was afflicted, and improve under it. My conformity to some customs which I believed were not right, were brought to my remembrance; and in the continuation of the exercise, I felt all the powers in me yield themselves up into the hands of Him who gave me being; and was made thankful that he had taken hold of me by his chastisement. Seeing the necessity of further purifying, there was now no desire in me for health, until the design of my correction was answered; and thus I lay in abasement and brokenness of spirit, and as I felt a sinking down into calm resignation, so I felt as in an instant, an inward healing in my nature; and from that time forward I grew better.

Though I was thus settled in mind in relation to hurtful dyes, I felt easy to wear my garments heretofore made; and so continued about nine months. Then I thought of getting a hat the natural color of the fur; but the apprehension of being looked upon as one affecting singularity, felt uneasy to me. Here I had occasion to consider, that things though small in themselves, being clearly enjoined by Divine authority, became great things to us; and I trusted that the Lord would support me in the trials that might attend singularity, while that singularity was only for his sake. On this account I was under close exercise of mind in the time of our General Spring Meeting in 1762, greatly desiring to be rightly directed; and being deeply bowed in spirit before the Lord, I was made willing to submit to what I apprehended was required of me;

and when I returned home, got a hat of the natural color of the fur.

In attending meetings this singularity was a trial upon me, and more especially at this time, white hats being used by some who were fond of following the changeable modes of dress; and as some Friends who knew not on what motives I wore it, carried shy of me, I felt my way for a time shut up in the exercise of the ministry. — In this condition my mind being turned toward my heavenly Father, with fervent cries that I might be preserved to walk before him in the meekness of wisdom, my heart was often tender in meetings; and I felt inward consolation, which to me was very precious under those difficulties.

I had several dyed garments fit for use, which I believed it best to wear till I had occasion for new ones.— Some Friends were apprehensive that my wearing such a hat savored of an affected singularity; and such who spoke with me in a friendly way, I generally informed in a few words, that I believed my wearing it was not in my own will. I had at times been sensible that a superficial friendship had been dangerous to me; and many Friends being now uneasy with me, I had an inclination to acquaint some with the manner of my being led into these things; yet upon a deeper thought I was for a time most easy to omit it, believing the present dispensation was profitable; and trusting that if I kept my place, the Lord in his own time would open the hearts of Friends toward me: since which I have had cause to admire his goodness and loving-kindness, in leading about and instructing, and opening and enlarging my heart in some of our meetings.

In the eleventh month of the year 1762, feeling an engagement of mind to visit some families in Mansfield, I joined my beloved friend Benjamin Jones, and we spent a few days together in that service. In the second month, 1763, I joined in company with Elizabeth Smith and Mary Noble, on a visit to the families of Friends at Ancocas; in both which visits, through the baptizing power of Truth, the sincere laborers were often comforted, and the hearts of Friends opened to receive us. In the fourth month following, I accompanied some Friends in a visit to the families of Friends in Mount Holly; in which my mind was often drawn into an inward awfulness, wherein strong desires were raised for the everlasting welfare of my fellow-creatures; and through the kindness of our heavenly Father, our hearts were at times enlarged, and Friends invited in the flowings of Divine love to attend to that which would settle them on the sure foundation.

Having many years felt love in my heart toward the natives of this land, who dwell far back in the wilderness, whose ancestors were the owners and possessors of the land where we dwell; and who for a very small consideration, assigned their inheritance to us; and being at Philadelphia in the eighth month, 1761, on a visit to some Friends who had slaves, I fell in company with some of those natives who lived on the east branch of the river Susquehanna, at an Indian town called Wehaloosing, two hundred miles from Philadelphia. In conversation with them by an interpreter, as also by observations on their countenances and conduct, I believed some of them were measurably acquainted with that Divine power which subjects the rough and froward will of the creature; and at times I felt inward drawings toward a visit to that place, of which I told none except my dear wife, until it came to some ripeness. In the winter of 1762, I laid it before Friends at our Monthly and Quarterly, and afterward at our General Spring Meeting; and having the unity of Friends, and being thoughtful about an Indian pilot, there came a man and three women from a little beyond that town to Philadelphia on business. Being informed thereof by letter, I met them in town in the fifth month, 1763; and after some conversation, finding they were sober people, with the concurrence of Friends in that place, I agreed to join them as companions in their return. On the 7th day of the sixth month following, we appointed to meet at Samuel Foulk's, at Richland, in Bucks county. As this visit felt weighty, and was performed at a time when travelling appeared perilous, so the dispensations of Divine Providence in preparing my mind for it, have been memorable; and I believe it good for me to give some hints thereof.

After I had given up to go, the thoughts of the journey were often attended with unusual sadness; in which times my heart was frequently turned to the Lord with inward breathings for his heavenly support, that I might not fail to follow him wheresoever he might lead me. — Being at our Youths' meeting at Chesterfield, about a week before the time I expected to set off, I was there led to speak on that prayer of our Redeemer to his Father: "I pray not that thou shouldst keep them out of the world, but that thou shouldst keep them from the evil." In attending to the pure openings of Truth, I had to mention what he elsewhere said to his Father: "I know that thou hearest me at all times": so that as some of his followers kept their places, and as his prayer was granted, it followed necessarily that they were kept from evil. As some of those met with great hardships and afflictions in this world, and at last suffered death by cruel men, it appears that whatsoever befalls men while they live in pure obedience to God, as it certainly works for their good, so it may not be considered an evil as it relates to them. As I spoke on this subject, my heart was much tendered, and great awfulness came over me; and on the first-day of the next week, at our own afternoon meeting, my heart being enlarged in love, I was led to speak on the care and protection of the Lord over his people, and to make mention of that passage where a band of Assyrians, endeavoring to take the prophet captive, were disappointed; and how the psalmist said, "the angel of the Lord encampeth round about them that fear him." I parted from Friends in true love and tenderness, expecting the next morning to proceed on my journey; and being weary, went early to bed: and after I had been asleep a short time, I was awaked by a man calling at my door; and arising, was invited to meet some Friends at a public house in our town, who came from Philadelphia so late that Friends were generally gone to bed. These Friends informed me that an express arrived the last morning from Pittsburgh, and brought news that the Indians had taken a fort from the English westward, and slain and scalped English people in divers places, some near Pittsburgh; and that some elderly Friends in Philadelphia, knowing the time of my expecting to set off, had conferred together, and thought good to inform me of these things before I left home, that I might consider them and proceed as I believed best. I went to bed again, and told not my wife till morning. My heart was turned to the Lord for his heavenly instruction; and it was an humbling time to me. When I told my dear wife, she appeared to be deeply concerned about it; but in a few hours' time, my mind became settled in a belief that it was my duty to proceed on my journey; and she bore it with a good degree of resignation. In this conflict of spirit, there were great searchings of heart and strong cries to the Lord, that no motion might be in the least degree attended to, but that of the pure Spirit of Truth.

The subjects before mentioned, on which I had so lately spoken in public, were now very fresh before me; and I was brought inwardly to commit myself to the Lord, to be disposed of as he saw best. I took leave of my family and neighbors in much bowedness of spirit, and went to our Monthly Meeting at Burlington; and after taking leave of Friends there, I crossed the river, accompanied by my friends Israel and John Pemberton; and parting the next morning with Israel, John bore me company to Samuel Foulk's; where I met the before-mentioned Indians, and we were glad to see each other. Here my friend Benjamin Parvin met me, and proposed joining as a companion, we having passed some letters before on the subject; and now on his account I had a sharp trial; for as the journey appeared perilous, I thought if he went chiefly to bear me company, and we should be taken captive, my having been the means of drawing him into these difficulties would add to my own afflictions. So I told him my mind freely, and let him know that I was resigned to go alone; but after all, if he really believed it to be his duty to go on, I believed his company would be very comfortable to me. It was indeed a time of deep exercise, and Benjamin appeared to be so fastened to the visit, that he could not be easy to leave me; so we went on, accompanied by our friends John Pemberton and William Lightfoot, of Pikeland, and lodged at Bethlehem. Parting there with John, William and we went forward on the 9th day of the sixth month, and got lodging on the floor of a house about five miles from Fort Allen. Here we parted with William. At this place we met with an Indian trader, lately come from Wyoming; and in conversation with him, I perceived that white people often sell rum to the Indians, which I believe is a great evil; first, they being thereby deprived of the use of their reason, and their spirits violently agitated, quarrels often arise which end in mischief; and the bitterness and resentments occasioned hereby, are frequently of long continuance. Again, their skins and furs, gotten through much fatigue and hard travels in hunting, with which they intended to buy clothing, when they become intoxicated, they often sell at a low rate for more rum; and afterward, when they suffer for want of the necessaries of life, are angry with those who, for the sake of gain, took the advantage of their weakness. Of this their chiefs have often complained, at their treaties with the English. Where cunning people pass counterfeits, and impose that on others which is good for nothing, it is considered as a wickedness; but to sell that to people which we know does them harm, and which often works their ruin, for the sake of gain, manifests a hardened and corrupt heart; and is an evil which demands the care of all true lovers of virtue to suppress. While my mind this evening was thus employed, I also remembered that the people on the frontiers, among whom this evil is too common, are often poor; who venture to the outside of a colony, that they may live more independently of such who are wealthy, who often set high rents on their land. I was renewedly confirmed in a belief, that if all our inhabitants lived according to sound wisdom, laboring to promote universal love and righteousness, and ceased from every inordinate desire after wealth, and from all customs which are tinctured with luxury, the way would be easy for the inhabitants, though much more numerous than at present, to live comfortably on honest employments, without that temptation they are often under of being drawn into schemes to make settlements on lands which have not been purchased of the Indians, or of applying to that wicked practice of selling rum to them.

On the 10th day of the month we set out early in the morning, and crossed the western branch of the Delaware, called the Great Lehigh, near Fort Allen; the water being high, we went over in a canoe. Here we met an Indian, and had some friendly conversation with him, and gave him some biscuit; and he having killed a deer, gave the Indians with us some of it. After travelling some miles, we met several Indian men and women with a cow and horse and some household goods, who were lately come from their dwelling at Wyoming, and going to settle at another place; we made them some small presents; and some of them understanding English, I told them my motive in coming into their country; with which they appeared satisfied. One of our guides talking a while with an ancient woman concerning us, the poor old woman came to my companion and me, and took her leave of us with an appearance of sincere affection. So going on we pitched our tent near the banks of the same river, having labored hard in crossing some of those mountains called the Blue Ridge; and by the roughness of the stones and the cavities between them, and the steepness of the hills, it appeared dangerous: but we were preserved in safety, through the kindness of Him whose works in those mountainous deserts appeared awful; toward whom my heart was turned during this day's travel.

Near our tent, on the sides of large trees peeled for that purpose, were various representations of men going to and returning from the wars, and of some killed in battle. This being a path heretofore used by warriors, and as I walked about viewing those Indian histories, which were painted mostly in red but some in black, and thinking on the innumerable afflictions which the proud, fierce spirit produceth in the world; thinking on the toils and fatigues of warriors, travelling over mountains and deserts; thinking on their miseries and distresses when wounded far from home by their enemies; and of their bruises and great weariness in chasing one another over the rocks and mountains; and of their restless, unquiet state of mind, who live in this spirit; and of the hatred which mutually grows up in the minds of the children of those nations engaged in war with each other: during these meditations, the desire to cherish the spirit of love and peace amongst these people, arose very fresh in me. This was the first night that we lodged in the woods; and being wet with travelling in the rain, the ground, our tent, and the bushes which we purposed to lay under our blankets also wet, all looked discouraging; but I believed that it was the Lord who had thus far brought me forward, and that he would dispose of me as he saw good, and therein I felt easy. We kindled a fire with our tent open to it; and with some bushes next the ground, and then our blankets, we made our bed; and lying down, got some sleep: and in the morning feeling a little unwell, I went into the river; the water was cold, but soon after I felt fresh and well.

The 11th day of the sixth month, the bushes being wet, we tarried in our tent till about eight o'clock; when going on, crossed a high mountain supposed to be upward of four miles over; the steepness of the north side exceeding all the others: we also crossed two swamps; and it raining near night, we pitched our tent and lodged.

About noon, on our way we were overtaken by one of the Moravian brethren going to Wehaloosing, and an Indian man with him who could talk English; and we being together while our horses eat grass, had some friendly conversation; but they travelling faster than we, soon left us. This Moravian I understood had spent some time this spring at Wehaloosing; and was by some of the Indians invited to come again.

The 12th day of the sixth month, and first of the week, it being rainy, we continued in our tent; and here I was led to think on the nature of the exercise which hath attended me. Love was the first motion, and thence a concern arose to spend some time with the Indians, that I might feel and understand their life and the spirit they live in, if haply I might receive some instruction from them, or they be in any degree helped forward by my following the leadings of Truth amongst them. As it pleased the Lord to make way for my going at a time when the troubles of war were increasing, and by reason of much wet weather, travelling was more difficult than usual, I looked upon it as a more favorable opportunity to season my mind, and bring me into a nearer sympathy with them: and as mine eye was to the great Father of mercies, humbly desiring to learn what his will was concerning me, I was made quiet and content.

Our guide's horse, though hoppled, went away in the night; and after finding our own, and searching some time for him, his footsteps were discovered in the path going back again, whereupon my kind companion went off in the rain, and after about seven hours returned with him: we lodged here again; tying up our horses before we went to bed, and loosing them to feed about break of day.

On the 13th day of the sixth month, the sun appearing, we set forward; and as I rode over the barren hills, my meditations were on the alteration in the circumstances of the natives of this land since the coming of the English. The lands near the sea are conveniently situated for fishing; the lands near the rivers where the tides flow, and some above, are in many places fertile, and not mountainous; while the running of the tides makes passing up and down easy with any kind of traffic. Those natives have in some places, for trifling considerations, sold their inheritance so favorably situated; and in other places been driven back by superior force: so that in many places as their way of clothing themselves is now altered from what it was, and they are far remote from us, they have to pass over mountains, swamps and barren deserts, where travelling is very troublesome, in bringing their skins and furs to trade with us.

By the extending of English settlements, and partly by English hunters, the wild beasts they chiefly depend on for a subsistence are not so plenty as they were; and people too often, for the sake of gain, open a door for them to waste their skins and furs, in purchasing a liquor which tends to the ruin of them and their families.

My own will and desires being now very much broken, my heart with much earnestness turned to the Lord, to whom alone I looked for help in the dangers before me. I had a prospect of the English along the coast, for upwards of nine hundred miles, where I have travelled; and their favorable situation and the difficulties attending the natives in many places, and also the negroes, were open before me; and a weighty and heavenly care came over my mind, and love filled my heart toward all mankind, in which I felt a strong engagement that we might be obedient to the Lord, while in tender mercies he is yet calling to us; and so attend to pure universal righteousness, as to give no just cause of offence to the Gentiles who do not profess Christianity, whether the blacks from Africa or the native inhabitants of this continent. I was led into a close, laborious inquiry, whether as an individual I kept clear from all things which tended to stir up, or were connected with wars, either in this land or Africa; and my heart was deeply concerned, that in future I might in all things keep steadily to the pure Truth, and live and walk in the plainness and simplicity of a sincere follower of Christ. In this lonely journey this day, I did greatly bewail the spreading of a wrong spirit, believing that the prosperous, convenient situation of the English, requires a constant attention to Divine love and wisdom to guide and support us in a way answerable to the will of that good, gracious and Almighty Being, who hath an equal regard to all mankind. Here, luxury and covetousness, with the numerous oppressions and other evils attending them, appeared very afflicting to me; and I felt in that which is immutable, that the seeds of great calamity and desolation are sown and growing fast on this continent: nor have I words sufficient to set forth the longing I then felt, that we who are placed along the coast, and have tasted the love and goodness of God, might arise in his strength; and like faithful messengers, labor to check the growth of these seeds, that they may not ripen to the ruin of our posterity.

We reached the Indian settlement at Wyoming,° and were told that an Indian runner had been at that place a day or two before us, and brought news of the Indians taking an English fort westward and destroying the people, and that they were endeavoring to take another; and also that another Indian runner came there about the middle of the night before we got there, who came from a town about ten miles above Wehaloosing, and brought news that some Indian warriors from distant parts came to that town with two English scalps; and told the people that it was war with the English.

Our guides took us to the house of a very ancient man; and soon after we had put in our baggage, there came a man from another Indian house some distance off, and I perceiving there was a man near the door, went out; and he having a tomahawk under his matchcoat out of sight, as I approached him he took it in his hand. I however went forward, and speaking to him in a friendly way perceived he understood some English: my companion then coming out, we had some talk with him concerning the nature of our visit in these parts; and then he going into the house with us, and talking with our guides, soon appeared friendly, and sat down and smoked his pipe. Though his taking his hatchet in his hand at the instant I drew near to him had a disagreeable appearance, I believe he had no other intent than to be in readiness in case any violence was offered to him.

Hearing the news brought by these Indian runners, and being told where we lodged that the Indians living about Wyoming expected in a few days to move to some larger towns, I thought that, to all outward appearance, it was dangerous travelling at this time. After a hard day's journey, I was brought into a painful exercise at night, in which I had to trace back and view over the steps I had taken from my first moving in the visit; and though I had to bewail some weakness which at times had attended me, yet I could not find that I had ever given way to a wilful disobedience. As I believed I had under a sense of duty come thus far, I was now earnest in spirit beseeching the Lord to show me what I ought to do. In this great distress I grew jealous of myself, lest the desire of reputation, as a man firmly settled to persevere through dangers, or the fear of disgrace arising on my returning without performing the visit, might have some place in me. Thus I lay full of thoughts during a great part of the night, while my beloved companion lay and slept by me; until the Lord, my gracious Father, who saw the conflicts of my soul, was pleased to give me quietness. I was again strengthened to commit my life and all things relating thereto into his heavenly hands; and getting a little sleep toward day, when morning came we arose.

On the 14th day of the sixth month, we sought out and visited all the Indians hereabouts that we could meet with; they being chiefly in one place, about a mile from where we lodged, in all perhaps twenty. I expressed the care I had on my mind for their good; and told them that true love had made me willing thus to leave my family to come and see the Indians, and speak with them in their houses. Some of them appeared kind and friendly. We took our leave of these Indians, and went up the river Susquehanna about three miles, to the house of an Indian called Jacob January, who had killed his hog; and the women were making a store of bread, and preparing to move up the river. Here our pilots left their canoe when they came down in the spring, which lying dry, was leaky; so that we being detained some hours, had a good deal of friendly conversation with the family, and eating dinner with them, made them some small presents. Then putting our baggage in the canoe, some of them pushed slowly up the stream, and the rest of us rode our horses; and swimming them over a creek called Lahawahamunk, we pitched our tent a little above it, there being a shower in the evening: and in a sense of God's goodness in helping me in my distress, sustaining me under trials and inclining my heart to trust in him, I lay down in an humble bowed frame of mind, and had a comfortable night's lodging.

On the 15th day of the sixth month, we proceeded forward until the afternoon; when a storm appearing, we met our canoe at an appointed place, and staid there all night; the rain continuing so heavy, that it beat through our tent and wet us and our baggage.

On the 16th day, we found on our way an abundance of trees blown down with the storm yesterday; and had occasion reverently to consider the kind dealings of the Lord, who provided a safe place for us in a valley, while this storm continued. By the falling of trees across our path we were much hindered, and in some swamps our way was so stopped, that we got through with extreme difficulty.

I had this day often to consider myself as a sojourner in the world; and a belief in the all-sufficiency of God to support his people in their pilgrimage felt comfortable to me; and I was industriously employed to get to a state of perfect resignation.

We seldom saw our canoe but at appointed places, by reason of the path going off from the river: and this afternoon, Job Chilaway, an Indian from Wehaloosing, who talks good English, and is acquainted with several people in and about Philadelphia, met our people on the river; and understanding where we expected to lodge, pushed back about six miles, and came to us after night; and in a while our own canoe came, it being hard work pushing up stream. Job told us that an Indian came in haste to their town yesterday, and told them that three warriors, coming from some distance, lodged in a town above Wehaloosing a few nights past; and that these three men were going against the English at Juniata. Job was going down the river to the province store at Shamokin. Though I was so far favored with health as to continue travelling, yet through the various difficulties in our journey, and the different way of living from what I had been used to, I grew sick: and the news of these warriors being on their march so near us, and not knowing whether we might not fall in with them, was a fresh trial of my faith; and though, through the strength of Divine love, I had several times been enabled to commit myself to the Divine disposal, I still found the want of my strength being renewed, that I might persevere therein; and my cries for help were put up to the Lord, who in great mercy gave me a resigned heart, in which I found quietness.

On the 17th day, parting from Job Chilaway, we went on and reached Wehaloosing about the middle of the afternoon; and the first Indian we saw was a woman of a modest countenance, with a Bible, who first spoke to our guide; and then with a harmonious voice expressed her gladness at seeing us, having before heard of our coming. By the direction of our guide we sat down on a log, and he went to the town to tell the people we were come. My companion and I sitting thus together, in a deep inward stillness, the poor woman came and sat near us; and great awfulness coming over us, we rejoiced in a sense of God's love manifested to our poor souls. After a while we heard a conk-shell blow several times, and then came John Curtis and another Indian man, who kindly invited us into a house near the town, where we found, I suppose, about sixty people sitting in silence. After sitting a short time, I stood up and in some tenderness of spirit acquainted them with the nature of my visit, and that a concern for their good had made me willing to come thus far to see them; all in a few short sentences, which some of them understanding, interpreted to the others, and there appeared gladness amongst them. Then I showed them my certificate, which was explained to them; and the Moravian who overtook us on the way, being now here, bade me welcome.

On the 18th day we rested ourselves in the forenoon; and the Indians knowing that the Moravian and I were of different religious societies, and that some of their people had encouraged him to come and stay awhile with them, were I believe concerned, that no jarring or discord might be in their meetings; and they I suppose, having conferred together, acquainted me that the people at my request, would at any time come together and hold meetings; and also told me, that they expected the Moravian would speak in their settled meetings, which are commonly held morning and near evening. I found a liberty in my heart to speak to the Moravian, and told him of the care I felt on my mind for the good of these people; and that I believed no ill effects would follow, if I sometimes spoke in their meetings when love engaged me thereto, without calling them together at times when they did not meet of course: whereupon he expressed his good-will toward my speaking at any time, all that I found in my heart to say. Near evening I was at their meeting, where the pure Gospel love was felt, to the tendering some of our hearts; and the interpreters endeavoring to acquaint the people with what I said in short sentences, found some difficulty, as none of them were quite perfect in the English and Delaware tongues, so they helped one another, and we labored along, Divine love attending. Afterward, feeling my mind covered with the spirit of prayer, I told the interpreters that I found it in my heart to pray to God, and believed if I prayed aright, he would hear me, and expressed my willingness for them to omit interpreting; so our meeting ended with a degree of Divine love. Before the people went out, I observed Papunehang, a man who had been zealous in laboring for a reformation in that town, being then very tender, spoke to one of the interpreters; and I was afterward told that he said in substance; "I love to feel where words come from."

On the 19th day and first of the week, this morning in the meeting the Indian who came with the Moravian, being also a member of that society, prayed; and then the Moravian spoke a short time to the people. In the afternoon they coming together, and my heart being filled with a heavenly care for their good, I spoke to them awhile by interpreters; but none of them being perfect in the work, and I feeling the current of love run strong, told the interpreters that I believed some of the people would understand me, and so I proceeded. In which exercise, I believe the Holy Ghost wrought on some hearts to edification, where all the words were not understood. I looked upon it as a time of Divine favor, and my heart was tendered and truly thankful before the Lord; and after I sat down, one of the interpreters seemed spirited to give the Indians the substance of what I had said.

Before our first meeting this morning, I was led to meditate on the manifold difficulties of these Indians; who, by the permission of the Six Nations,° dwell in these parts; and a near sympathy with them was raised in me; and my heart being enlarged in the love of Christ, I thought that the affectionate care of a good man for his only brother in affliction, did not exceed what I then felt for that people.

I came to this place through much trouble; and though through the mercies of God, I believed that if I died in the journey, it would be well with me; yet the thoughts of falling into the hands of Indian warriors, were in times of weakness afflicting to me; and being of a tender constitution, the thoughts of captivity amongst them, were at times grievous; supposing that they being strong and hardy, might demand service of me beyond what I could well bear; but the Lord alone was my keeper; and I believed if I went into captivity it would be for some good end; and thus from time to time, my mind was centred in resignation, in which I always found quietness. And now, this day, though I had the same dangerous wilderness between me and home, I was inwardly joyful that the Lord had strengthened me to come on this visit, and manifested a fatherly care over me in my poor lowly condition, when in mine own eyes I appeared inferior to many amongst the Indians.

When the last-mentioned meeting was ended, it being night, Papunehang went to bed; and one of the interpreters sitting by me, I observed Papunehang spoke with an harmonious voice, I suppose, a minute or two: and asking the interpreter, was told that "he was expressing his thankfulness to God for the favors he had received that day; and prayed that he would continue to favor him with the same which he had experienced in that meeting." That though Papunehang had before agreed to receive the Moravians, and join with them, he still appeared kind and loving to us.

On the 20th day I was at two meetings, and silent in them.

The 21st day. This morning in meeting my heart was enlarged in pure love amongst them, and in short plain sentences expressed several things that rested upon me, which one of the interpreters gave the people pretty readily; after which the meeting ended in supplication, and I had cause humbly to acknowledge the loving-kindness of the Lord toward us; and believed that a door remained open for the faithful disciples of Jesus Christ, to labor amongst these people.

Feeling my mind at liberty to return, I took my leave of them in general, at the conclusion of what I said in meeting; and so we prepared to go homeward: but some of their most active men told us, that when we were ready to move, the people would choose to come and shake hands with us; which those who usually come to meeting did; and from a secret draught in my mind, I went amongst some who did not use to go to meeting, and took my leave of them also: the Moravian and his Indian interpreter appeared respectful to us at parting. This town stands on the bank of Susquehanna, and consists, I believe, of about forty houses, mostly compact together; some about thirty feet long, and eighteen wide; some larger, some less; mostly built of split plank, one end set in the ground, and the other pinned to a plate, on which lay rafters covered with bark. I understand a great flood last winter overflowed the chief part of the ground where the town stands, and some were now about moving their houses to higher ground.

We expected only two Indians to be our company; but when we were ready to go, we found many of them were going to Bethlehem with skins and furs, who chose to go in company with us; so they loaded two canoes, which they desired us to go in, telling us, the waters were so raised with the rains, that the horses should be taken by persons who were better acquainted with the fording places: so we with several Indians went in the canoes, and others went on horses, there being seven besides ours. We met with the horsemen once on the way by appointment, a little below a stream called Tunkhannock: we lodged there, and some of the young men going out a little before dusk with their guns, brought in a deer.

On the 22d day, through diligence we reached Wyoming before night, and understood the Indians were mostly gone from this place: here we went up a small creek into the woods with our canoes, and pitching our tent, carried out our baggage; and before dark our horses came to us.

On the 23d day, in the morning, their horses were loaded, and we prepared our baggage and set forward, being in all fourteen; and with diligent travelling were favored to get nearly half way to Fort Allen. The land on this road from Wyoming to our frontier being mostly poor, and good grass scarce, they chose a piece of low ground to lodge on, as the best for grazing; and I having sweat much in travelling, and being weary, slept sound. I perceived in the night that I had taken cold, of which I was favored to get better soon.

On the 24th day we passed Fort Allen, and lodged near it in the woods.

We forded the westerly branch of the Delaware three times, and thereby had a shorter way, and missed going over the top of the Blue Mountains, called the Second Ridge. In the second time fording, where the river cuts through the mountain, the waters being rapid and pretty deep, and my companion's mare being a tall tractable animal, he sundry times drove her through the river, and they loaded her with the burthens of some small horses, which they thought not sufficient to come through with their loads.

The troubles westward, and the difficulty for Indians to pass through our frontier, I apprehend was one reason why so many came; expecting that our being in company would prevent the frontier inhabitants from being surprised.

On the 25th day we reached Bethlehem, taking care on the way to keep foremost, and to acquaint people on and near the road who these Indians were: this we found very needful; for the frontier inhabitants were often alarmed at the report of English being killed by Indians westward.

Amongst our company were some who I did not remember

to have seen at meeting, and some of these at first were very reserved; but we being several days together, and behaving friendly toward them, and making them suitable returns for the services they did us, they became more free and sociable.

On the 26th day, and first of the week, having carefully endeavored to settle all affairs with the Indians relative to our journey, we took leave of them, and I thought they generally parted with us affectionately. We got to Richland, and had a very comfortable meeting amongst our friends: here I parted with my kind friend and companion Benjamin Parvin; and accompanied by my friend Samuel Foulk, we rode to John Cadwallader's, from whence I reached home the next day, where I found my family middling well; and they and my friends all along appeared glad to see me return from a journey which they apprehended dangerous. My mind while I was out, had been so employed in striving for a perfect resignation, and I had so often been confirmed in a belief that whatever the Lord might be pleased to allot for me would work for good, that I was careful lest I should admit any degree of selfishness in being glad overmuch, and labored to improve by those trials in such a manner as my gracious Father and protector intends for me. Between the English settlements and Wehaloosing, we had only a narrow path, which in many places is much grown up with bushes, and interrupted by abundance of trees lying across it; these, together with the mountains, swamps and rough stones, make it a difficult road to travel; and the more so, for that rattlesnakes abound there, of which we killed four. People who have never been in such places, have but an imperfect idea of them; but I was not only taught patience, but also made thankful to God, who thus led me about and instructed me, that I might have a quick and lively feeling of the afflictions of my fellow-creatures whose situation in life is difficult.

CHAPTER IX

His religious conversation with a company met to see the tricks of a juggler — John Smith's advice; proceedings of a committee at the Yearly Meeting in 1764 — Contemplations on the nature of true wisdom, occasioned by hearing of the cruelty of the Indians to their captives — Visits the families of Friends at Mount Holly, Mansfield and Burlington, in 1764, and the meetings on the sea coast from Cape May toward Squan in 1765 — Visit to the lower counties on Delaware and the Eastern Shore of Maryland in 1766, in company with John Sleeper; some account of Joseph Nichols and his followers; and observations on the different state of the first settlers in Pennsylvania who depended on their own labor, and those of the Southern provinces who kept negroes — Visit to the northern parts of New Jersey the same year, and the western parts of Maryland and Pennsylvania in 1767, and afterward other parts of Pennsylvania and the families of Friends at Mount Holly; and again several parts of Maryland in 1768 — Further considerations on keeping slaves; his concern for having formerly, as an executor, been party to the sale of one; and what he did in consequence of it — Thoughts on Friends exercising offices in civil government.

The latter part of the summer of 1763, there came a man to Mount Holly, who had before published by a printed advertisement, that at a certain public house he would show many wonderful operations, which he therein enumerated.

This man at the time appointed, did, by sleight of hand, sundry things, which to those gathered, appeared strange.

I heard of it next day, and understanding that the show was to be continued the next night, and the people to meet about sunset, I felt an exercise on that account: so I went to the public house in the evening, and told the man of the house that I had an inclination to spend a part of the evening there; with which he signified that he was content. Then sitting down by the door, I spoke to the people as they came together, concerning this show; and more coming and sitting down with us, the seats at the door were mostly filled; and I had conversation with them in the fear of the Lord, and labored to convince them that thus assembling to see those tricks or sleights of hand, and bestowing their money to support men who in that capacity were of no use in the world, was contrary to the nature of the Christian religion.

There was one of the company who, for a time, endeavored by arguments to show the reasonableness of their proceedings; but after considering some texts of Scripture and calmly debating the matter, he gave up the point. Having spent about an hour amongst them, and feeling my mind easy, I departed.

At our Yearly Meeting in Philadelphia, on the 25th day of the ninth month, 1764, John Smith of Marlborough, aged upwards of eighty years, a faithful minister, though not eloquent, stood up in our meeting of ministers and elders, and appearing to be under a great exercise of spirit, informed Friends in substance as follows, to wit: "That he had been a member of the Society upward of sixty years, and well remembered that in those early times Friends were a plain lowly-minded people; and that there was much tenderness and contrition in their meetings. — That at twenty years from that time, the Society increasing in wealth, and in some degree conforming to the fashions of the world, true humility was less apparent, and their meetings in general not so lively and edifying — that at the end of forty years, many of them were grown very rich; that wearing fine costly garments, and using silver and other watches, became customary with them, their sons and their daughters, and many of the Society made a specious appearance in the world; which marks of outward wealth and greatness, appeared on some in our meetings of ministers and elders; and as these things became more prevalent, so the powerful overshadowings of the Holy Ghost were less manifest in the Society — that there had been a continued increase of these ways of life even until now; and that the weakness which hath overspread the Society, and the barrenness manifest amongst us, is matter of much sorrow." He then mentioned the uncertainty of his attending these meetings in future, expecting his dissolution was now near; and having tenderly expressed his concern for us, signified that he had seen in the true light that the Lord would bring back his people from these things into which they were thus degenerated, but that his faithful servants must first go through great and heavy exercises.

On the 29th day, the committee appointed by the Yearly Meeting to visit the Quarterly and Monthly Meetings, gave an account in writing of their proceedings in that service; in which they signified, that in the course of it, they had been apprehensive that some persons holding offices in government, inconsistent with our principles; and others who kept slaves, remaining active members in our meetings of discipline, had been one means of weakness more and more prevailing in the management thereof in some places. After this report was read, an exercise revived on my mind, which at times had attended me for several years, and inward cries to the Lord were raised in me, that the fear of man might not prevent me from doing what he required of me; and standing up, I spoke in substance as follows: "I have felt a tenderness in my mind toward persons, in two circumstances mentioned in that report; that is, toward such active members who keep slaves, and such who hold offices in civil government; and have desired, that Friends in all their conduct may be kindly affectioned one toward another. Many Friends who keep slaves, are under some exercise on that account; and at times, think about trying them with freedom; but find many things in their way. The way of living, and annual expenses of some of them are such, that it seems impracticable for them to set their slaves free, without changing their own way of life. It has been my lot to be often abroad; and I have observed in some places, at Quarterly and Yearly Meetings, and at some houses where travelling Friends and their horses are often entertained, that the yearly expense of individuals therein is very considerable. Friends in some places crowding much on persons in these circumstances for entertainment, hath often rested as a burthen on my mind for some years past, and I now express it in the fear of the Lord, greatly desiring that Friends now present may duly consider it."

In the fall of this year having hired a man to work, I perceived in conversation that he had been a soldier in the late war on this continent; and in the evening giving a narrative of his captivity amongst the Indians, he informed me that he saw two of his fellow-captives tortured to death in a very cruel manner.

This relation affected me with sadness, under which I went to bed; and the next morning, soon after I awoke, a fresh and living sense of Divine love was spread over my mind; in which I had a renewed prospect of the nature of that wisdom from above, which leads to a right use of all gifts, both spiritual and temporal, and gives contentment therein: under a feeling thereof, I wrote as follows.

"Hath He, who gave me a being attended with many wants unknown to brute creatures, given me a capacity superior to theirs, and shown me, that a moderate application to business is proper to my present condition; and that this, attended with his blessing, may supply all outward wants, while they remain within the bounds he hath fixed; and no imaginary wants proceeding from an evil spirit, have any place in me? Attend them, O my soul! to this pure wisdom, as thy sure conductor through the manifold dangers in this world!

"Doth pride lead to vanity? Doth vanity form imaginary wants? Do these wants prompt men to exert their power in requiring that of others, from which they would rather be excused, were the same required of them?

"Do these proceedings beget hard thoughts? Do hard thoughts, when ripe, become malice! Does malice, when ripe, become revengeful; and in the end inflict terrible pains on their fellow-creatures, and spread desolations in the world?

"Do mankind, walking in uprightness, delight in each other's happiness? And do these creatures, capable of this attainment, by giving way to an evil spirit, employ their wit and strength to afflict and destroy one another?

"Remember then, O my soul! the quietude of those in whom Christ governs, and in all thy proceedings feel after it!

"Doth he condescend to bless thee with his presence? To move and influence to action? To dwell in thee and walk in thee? Remember then thy station, as a being sacred to God; accept of the strength freely offered thee; and take heed that no weakness, in conforming to expensive, unwise, and hard-hearted customs, gendering to discord and strife, be given way to. Doth he claim my body as his temple? And graciously grant that I may be sacred to him. Oh! that I may prize this favor; and that my whole life may be conformable to this character!

"Remember, O my soul! that the prince of peace is thy Lord: that he communicates his unmixed wisdom to his family; that they living in perfect simplicity, may give no just cause of offence to any creature, but may walk as he walked!"

Having felt an openness in my heart toward visiting families in our own meeting, and especially in the town of Mount Holly, the place of my abode, I mentioned it in our Monthly Meeting the fore part of the winter 1764; which being agreed to, and several Friends of our meeting being united in the exercise, we proceeded therein; and through Divine favor were helped in the work, so that it appeared to me as a fresh reviving of godly care amongst Friends. In the latter part of the same winter, I joined my friend William Jones, in a visit to Friends' families in Mansfield; in which labor I had cause to admire the goodness of the Lord toward us.

Having felt my mind drawn to visit Friends along the sea coast from Cape May to near Squan; and also to visit some people in those parts, amongst whom there is no settled worship; I joined with my beloved friend Benjamin Jones, in a visit there, having Friends' unity therein. We set off the 24th day of the tenth month, 1765, and had a prosperous and very satisfactory journey; feeling at times, through the goodness of the heavenly Shepherd, the Gospel to flow freely toward a poor people scattered in those places. Soon after our return, I joined my friends John Sleeper and Elizabeth Smith, in visiting Friends' families at Burlington, there being at this time about fifty families of our Society in that city; and we had cause humbly to adore our heavenly Father, who baptized us into a feeling of the state of the people, and strengthened us to labor in true Gospel love amongst them.

An exercise having at times for several years attended me, in regard to paying a religious visit to Friends on the Eastern Shore of Maryland; such was the nature of it, that I believed the Lord moved me to travel on foot amongst them, that by so doing I might have a more lively feeling of the condition of the oppressed slaves, set an example of lowliness before the eyes of their masters, and be more out of the way of temptation to unprofitable converse.

The time drawing near in which I believed it my duty to lay my concern before our Monthly Meeting, I perceived in conversation with my beloved friend John Sleeper, that he was under a concern to travel the same way, and also to go on foot in the form of a servant amongst them, as he expressed it. This he told me before he knew aught of my exercise.

We being thus drawn the same way, laid our exercise and the nature of it before Friends: and obtaining certificates, we set off the 6th day of the fifth month, 1766; and were at meetings with Friends at Wilmington, Duck Creek, Little Creek, and Motherkill; my heart being at times tendered under the Divine influence, and enlarged in love toward the people amongst whom we travelled.

From Motherkill, we crossed the country about thirty-five miles to Friends at Tuckahoe in Maryland, and had a meeting there and at Marshy Creek.

At these our three last meetings, were a considerable number of people, followers of one Joseph Nichols, a preacher; who, I understand, is not in outward fellowship with any religious society of people, but professes nearly the same principles as our Society doth, and often travels up and down appointing meetings, to which many people come. I heard Friends speaking of some of their neighbors, who had been irreligious people, that were now his followers, and were become sober well-behaved men and women.

Some irregularities I hear have been amongst the people at several of his meetings; but from the whole of what I have perceived, I believe the man and some of his followers, are honestly disposed, but that skilful fathers are wanting among them: from hence we went to Choptank and Third Haven; and thence to Queen Ann's. The weather for some days past having been hot and dry, and in order to attend meetings pursuant to appointment, we having travelled pretty steadily, and had hard labor in meetings, I grew weakly; at which I was for a time discouraged. But looking over our journey, and thinking how the Lord had supported our minds and bodies, so that we got forward much faster than I expected before we came out, I saw that I had been in danger of too strongly desiring to get soon through the journey, and that this bodily weakness was a kindness to me; and then in contrition of spirit, I became very thankful to my gracious Father, for this manifestation of his love; and in humble submission to his will, my trust was renewed in him.

On this part of our journey I had many thoughts on the different circumstances of Friends who inhabit Pennsylvania and Jersey, from those who dwell in Maryland, Virginia, and Carolina. Pennsylvania and New Jersey were settled by Friends who were convinced of our principles in England in times of suffering, and coming over bought lands of the natives, and applied themselves to husbandry in a peaceable way; and many of their children were taught to labor for their living.

Few Friends, I believe, came from England to settle in any of these Southern provinces; but by the faithful labors of travelling Friends in early times, there were considerable convincements amongst the inhabitants of these parts. Here I remembered my reading of the warlike disposition of many of the first settlers in these provinces, and of their numerous engagements with the natives, in which much blood was shed, even in the infancy of these colonies. The people inhabiting these places, being grounded in customs contrary to the pure Truth, when some of them were affected with the powerful preaching of the Word of Life, and joined in fellowship with our Society, they had a great work to go through. It is observable in the History of the Reformation from Popery, that it had a gradual progress from age to age. The uprightness of the first reformers, in attending to the light and understanding given them, opened the way for sincere-hearted people to proceed further afterward; and thus each one truly fearing God, and laboring in those works of righteousness appointed for them in their day, findeth acceptance with him. Through the darkness of the times and the corruption of manners and customs, some upright men may have had little more for their day's work than to attend to the righteous principle in their minds, as it related to their own conduct in life, without pointing out to others the whole extent of that, which the same principle would lead succeeding ages into. Thus, for instance; amongst an imperious warlike people, supported by oppressed slaves, some of these masters I suppose are awakened to feel and see their error; and through sincere repentance, cease from oppression and become like fathers to their servants; showing by their example, a pattern of humility in living and moderation in governing, for the instruction and admonition of their oppressing neighbors; those without carrying the reformation further, I believe have found acceptance with the Lord. Such was the beginning; and those who succeeded them, and have faithfully attended to the nature and spirit of the reformation, have seen the necessity of proceeding further; and not only to instruct others by their example of governing well, but also to use means to prevent their successors from having so much power to oppress others.

Here I was renewedly confirmed in my mind, that the Lord, whose tender mercies are over all his works, and whose ear is open to the cries and groans of the oppressed, is graciously moving on the hearts of people, to draw them off from the desire of wealth, and bring them into such an humble, lowly way of living, that they may see their way clearly, to repair to the standard of true righteousness; and not only break the yoke of oppression, but know him to be their strength and support in a time of outward affliction.

Passing on, we crossed Chester River, and had a meeting there, and at Cecil and Sassafras. Through my bodily weakness, joined with a heavy exercise of mind, it was to me an humbling dispensation, and I had a very lively feeling of the state of the oppressed; yet I often thought that what I suffered was little, compared with the sufferings of the blessed Jesus, and many of his faithful followers; and may say with thankfulness, I was made content.

From Sassafras we went pretty directly home, where we

found our families well; and for several weeks after our return, I had often to look over our journey; and though to me it appeared as a small service, and that some faithful messengers will yet have more bitter cups to drink for Christ's sake in those Southern provinces, than we had; yet I found peace in that I had been helped to walk in sincerity, according to the understanding and strength given me.

On the 13th day of the eleventh month, 1766, with the unity of Friends at our Monthly Meeting, in company with my beloved friend Benjamin Jones, I set out on a visit to Friends in the upper part of this province, having for a considerable time had drawings of love in my heart that way: we travelled as far as Hardwick; and I had inward peace in my labors of love amongst them.

Through the humbling dispensations of Divine Providence, my mind hath been brought into a further feeling of the difficulties of Friends and their servants south-westward: and being often engaged in spirit on their account, I believed it my duty to walk into some parts on the Western Shore of Maryland, on a religious visit. Having obtained a certificate from Friends of our Monthly Meeting, I took my leave of my family under the heart-tendering operation of Truth; and on the 20th day of the fourth month, 1767, I rode to the ferry opposite to Philadelphia, and from thence walked to William Horne's, at Darby, that evening; and next day pursued my journey alone, and reached Concord week-day meeting.

Discouragements and a weight of distress had at times attended me in this lonesome walk; through which afflictions I was mercifully preserved: and now sitting down with Friends, my mind was turned toward the Lord, to wait for his holy leadings; who, in infinite love, was pleased to soften my heart into humble contrition, and renewedly strengthen me to go forward; that to me it was a time of heavenly refreshment in a silent meeting.

The next day I came to New Garden week-day meeting, in which I sat with bowedness of spirit; and being baptized into a feeling of the state of some present, the Lord gave us an heart-tendering season; to his name be the praise.

I passed on, and was at Nottingham Monthly Meeting; and at a meeting at Little Britain on first-day: and in the afternoon several Friends came to the house where I lodged, and we had a little afternoon meeting; and through the humbling power of Truth, I had to admire the loving-kindness of the Lord manifested to us.

On the 26th day I crossed the Susquehanna; and coming amongst people living in outward ease and greatness, chiefly on the labor of slaves, my heart was much affected; and in awful retiredness, my mind was gathered inward to the Lord, being humbly engaged, that in true resignation I might receive instruction from him respecting my duty amongst this people.

Though travelling on foot was wearisome to my body, yet it was agreeable to the state of my mind.

I went gently on, being weakly; and was covered with sorrow and heaviness, on account of the spreading prevailing spirit of this world, introducing customs grievous and oppressive on one hand, and cherishing pride and wantonness on the other. In this lonely walk and state of abasement and humiliation, the state of the church in these parts was opened before me; and I may truly say with the prophet, "I was bowed down at the hearing of it; I was dismayed at the seeing of it." Under this exercise, I attended the Quarterly Meeting at Gunpowder; and in bowedness of spirit, I had to open with much plainness, what I felt respecting Friends living in fulness, on the labors of the poor oppressed negroes; and that promise of the Most High was now revived; "I will gather all nations and tongues; and they shall come and see my glory." Here the sufferings of Christ and his tasting death for every man, and the travels, sufferings and martyrdom of the apostles and primitive Christians, in laboring for the conversion of the Gentiles, was livingly revived in me; and according to the measure of strength afforded, I labored in some tenderness of spirit, being deeply affected amongst them. The difference between the present treatment which these Gentiles, the negroes, receive at our hands, and the labors of the primitive Christians for the conversion of the Gentiles, was pressed home, and the power of Truth came over us; under a feeling of which, my mind was united to a tender-hearted people in those parts; and the meeting concluded in a sense of God's goodness toward his humble dependent children.

The next day was a general meeting for worship, much crowded: in which I was deeply engaged in inward cries to the Lord for help, that I might stand wholly resigned, and move only as he might be pleased to lead me; and I was mercifully helped to labor honestly and fervently amongst them, in which I found inward peace; and the sincere were comforted.

From hence I turned toward Pipe Creek, and passed on to the Red Lands; and had several meetings amongst Friends in those parts. My heart was often tenderly affected, under a sense of the Lord's goodness, in sanctifying my troubles and exercises, turning them to my comfort, and I believe, to the benefit of many others; for I may say with thankfulness, that in this visit it appeared like a fresh tendering visitation in most places.

I passed on to the western Quarterly Meeting in Pennsylvania; during the several days of this meeting, I was mercifully preserved in an inward feeling after the mind of Truth, and my public labors tended to my humiliation, with which I was content. After the Quarterly Meeting of worship ended, I felt drawings to go to the women's meeting of business, which was very full; and here the humility of Jesus Christ, as a pattern for us to walk by, was livingly opened before me; and in treating on it my heart was enlarged, and it was a baptizing time. From hence I went on, and was at meetings at Concord, Middletown, Providence and Haddonfield, and so home; where I found my family well. A sense of the Lord's merciful preservation in this my journey, excites reverent thankfulness to him.

On the 2d day of the ninth month, 1767, with the unity of Friends, I set off on a visit to Friends in the upper part of Berks and Philadelphia counties; was at eleven meetings in about two weeks; and have renewed cause to bow in reverence before the Lord, who, by the powerful extendings of his humbling goodness, opened my way amongst Friends, and made the meetings, I trust, profitable to us. The following winter I joined in a visit to Friends' families in some part of our meeting; in which exercise, the pure influence of Divine love made our visits reviving.

On the 5th day of the fifth month, 1768, I left home under the humbling hand of the Lord, having obtained a certificate, in order to visit some meetings in Maryland; and to proceed without a horse looked clearest to me. I was at the Quarterly Meetings at Philadelphia and Concord; and then went on to Chester River; and crossing the bay with Friends, was at the Yearly Meeting at West River: thence back to Chester River; and taking a few meetings in my way, proceeded home. It was a journey of much inward waiting; and as my eye was to the Lord, way was several times opened to my humbling admiration, when things had appeared very difficult.

In my return I felt a relief of mind very comfortable to me; having, through Divine help, labored in much plainness, both with Friends selected, and in the more public meetings; so that I trust the pure witness in many minds was reached.

The 11th day of the sixth month, 1769. Sundry cases have happened of late years, within the limits of our Monthly Meeting, respecting the exercise of pure righteousness toward the negroes; in which I have lived under a labor of heart that equity might be steadily kept to. On this account I have had some close exercises amongst Friends; in which I may thankfully say, I find peace: and as my meditations have been on universal love, my own conduct in time past became of late very grievous to me.

As persons setting negroes free in our province are bound by law to maintain them, in case they have need of relief, some who scrupled keeping slaves for term of life, in the time of my youth, were wont to detain their young negroes in their service until thirty years of age, without wages, on that account: and with this custom I so far agreed, that being engaged with another Friend in executing the will of a deceased Friend, I once sold a negro lad till he might attain the age of thirty years, and applied the money to the use of the estate.

With abasement of heart I may now say, that sometimes as I have sat in meeting, with my heart exercised toward that awful Being, who respecteth not persons nor colors, and have looked upon this lad, I have felt that all was not clear in my mind respecting him: and as I have attended to this exercise, and fervently sought the Lord, it hath appeared to me that I should make some restitution, but in what way I saw not till lately. Being under a concern that I may be resigned to go on a visit to some part of the West Indies, and under close engagement of spirit, seeking to the Lord for counsel herein, my joining in the sale aforesaid came heavily upon me, and my mind for a time was covered with darkness and sorrow; and under this sore affliction, my heart was softened to receive instruction. Here I first saw, that as I had been one of the two executors, who had sold this lad nine years longer than is common for our own children to serve, so I should now offer a part of my substance to redeem the last half of that nine years; but as the time was not yet come, I executed a bond, binding me and my executors, to pay to the man he was sold to, what to candid men might appear equitable, for the last four years and a half of his time, in case the said youth should be living, and in a condition likely to provide comfortably for himself.

The 9th day of the tenth month, 1769. My heart hath often been deeply afflicted under a feeling I have had, that the standard of pure righteousness is not lifted up to the people by us as a Society, in that clearness which it might have been, had we been so faithful to the teachings of Christ as we ought to have been. As my mind hath been inward to the Lord, the purity of Christ's government hath been opened in my understanding; and under this exercise, that of Friends being active in civil society, in putting laws in force which are not agreeable to the purity of righteousness, hath for several years been an increasing burthen upon me. I have felt in the openings of universal love, that where a people, convinced of the truth of the inward teachings of Christ, are active in putting laws in execution which are not consistent with pure wisdom, it hath a necessary tendency to bring dimness over their minds: and as my heart hath been thus exercised, and a tender sympathy in me toward my fellow-members, I have within a few months past, in several meetings for discipline, expressed my concern on this subject.

CHAPTER X

His exercise for the good of the people in the West Indies — Communicates to Friends his resignation to visit some of these islands — The state of his mind, and the close considerations he was led into while under this exercise — Preparations to embark, and considerations on the trade to these islands; released from the concern he had been under — Religious engagements after his return home — His sickness, in which he was brought to a very low state; and the prospects he then had.

THE 12th day of the third month, 1770, having for some years past dieted myself on account of a lump gathering on my nose, I grew weak in body, and not of ability to travel by land as heretofore. I was at times favored to look with awfulness toward the Lord, before whom are all my ways, who alone hath the power of life and death; and to feel thankfulness raised in me, for this his fatherly chastisement, believing if I was truly humbled under it, all would work for good. While I was under this bodily weakness, my mind being at times exercised for my fellow-creatures in the West Indies, I grew jealous over myself, lest the disagreeableness of the prospect should hinder me from obediently attending thereto: for though I knew not that the Lord required me to go there, yet I believed that resignation was now called for in that respect. Feeling a danger of not being wholly devoted to him, I was frequently engaged to watch unto prayer, that I might be preserved; and upwards of a year having passed, as I walked one day into a solitary wood, my mind being covered with awfulness, cries were raised in me to my merciful Father, that he would graciously keep me in faithfulness; and it then settled on my mind as a duty, to open my condition to Friends at our Monthly Meeting; which I did soon after, as follows:—

"An exercise hath attended me for some time past, and of late been more weighty upon me, under which, I believe it is required of me to be resigned to go on a visit to some part of the West Indies." In the Quarterly and General Spring Meeting, I found no clearness to express anything further, than that I believed resignation herein was required of me; and having obtained certificates from all the said meetings, I felt like a sojourner at my outward habitation, kept free from worldly incumbrances, and was often bowed in spirit before the Lord, with inward breathings to him, that I might be rightly directed. I may here note, that what I have before related of my being, when young, joined as an executor with another Friend, in executing a will, our having sold a negro lad till he might attain the age of thirty years, was now the occasion of great sorrow to me. After having settled matters relating to this youth, I provided sea-stores, a bed, and other things for the voyage; and hearing of a vessel likely to sail from Philadelphia for Barbadoes, I spoke with one of the owners at Burlington, and soon after went to Philadelphia on purpose to speak with him again. He told me there was a Friend in town who was part owner of the said vessel; but I felt no inclination to speak with him, but returned home. A while after, I took leave of my family, and going to Philadelphia, had some weighty conversation with the first-mentioned owner, and showed him a writing, as follows:—

"On the 25th day of the eleventh month, 1769. As an exercise, with respect to a visit to Barbadoes, hath been weighty on my mind, I may express some of the trials which have attended me, under which, I have at times rejoiced that I have felt my own self-will subjected.

"Some years ago, I retailed rum, sugar and molasses, the fruits of the labor of slaves; but then had not much concern about them, save only that the rum might be used in moderation; nor was this concern so weightily attended to, as I now believe it ought to have been. But of late years being further informed respecting the oppressions too generally exercised in these islands, and thinking often on the degrees there are in the connections of interest and fellowship with the works of darkness, Ephe. v. 11; and feeling an increasing concern to be wholly given up to the leadings of the Holy Spirit, it hath appeared to me, that the small gain I got by this branch of trade, should be applied in promoting righteousness on the earth; and was the first motion toward a visit to Barbadoes. I believed the outward substance I possess should be applied in paying my passage, if I go, and providing things in a lowly way for my subsistence; but when the time drew near, in which I believed it required of me to be in readiness, a difficulty arose, which hath been a continued trial for some months past; under which, I have with abasement of mind, from day to day, sought the Lord for instruction; and often had a feeling of the condition of one formerly, who bewailed himself, for that the Lord hid his face from him. During these exercises, my heart hath been often contrite; and I have had a tender feeling of the temptations of my fellow-creatures, laboring under those expensive customs distinguishable from the simplicity that there is in Christ, 2 Cor. ii. 3, and sometimes in the renewings of Gospel love, I have been helped to minister to others.

"That which hath so closely engaged my mind in seeking to the Lord for instruction is, whether after so full information of the oppression which the slaves who raise the West India produce lie under (as I had in reading a caution and warning to Great Britain and her colonies, written by Anthony Benezet,) it is right for me to take a passage in a vessel employed in the West India trade.

"To trade freely with oppressors, and without laboring to dissuade from their unkind treatment, seek for gain by such traffic, tends, I believe, to make them more easy respecting their conduct, than they would be, if the cause of universal righteousness was humbly and firmly attended to by those with whom they have commerce. That complaint of the Lord by his prophet, 'They have strengthened the hands of the wicked,' hath very often revived in my mind; and I may here add some circumstances preceding any prospect of a visit there. The case of David hath often been before me of late years: he longed for some water in a well beyond an army of Philistines, at war with Israel; and some of his men, to please him, ventured their lives in passing through this army, and brought that water.

"It doth not appear that the Israelites were then scarce of water, but rather, that David gave way to delicacy of taste; but having thought on the danger these men were exposed to, he considered this water as their blood, and his heart smote him that he could not drink it, but poured it out to the Lord. The oppression of the slaves which I have seen in several journeys southward, on this continent, and the report of their treatment in the West Indies hath deeply affected me; and a care to live in the spirit of peace, and minister just cause of offence to none of my fellow-creatures, hath, from time to time, livingly revived on my mind; and under this exercise, I have for some years past, declined to gratify my palate with those sugars.

"I do not censure my brethren in these things; but believe the Father of mercies, to whom all mankind by creation are equally related, hath heard the groans of these oppressed people; and is preparing soon to have a tender feeling of their condition: and the trading in, or frequent use of any produce known to be raised by the labors of those who are under such lamentable oppression, hath appeared to be a subject which may yet require the more serious consideration of the humble followers of Christ, the prince of peace.

"After long and mournful exercise, I am now free to mention how things have opened in my mind, with desires that if it may please the Lord, further to open his will to any of his children in this matter, they may faithfully follow him in such further manifestation.

"The number of those who decline the use of the West India produce,° on account of the hard usage of the slaves who raise it, appears small, even amongst people truly pious; and the labors in Christian love on that subject, of those who do, are not very extensive.

"Were the trade from this continent to the West Indies to be quite stopped at once, I believe many there would suffer for want of bread.

"Did we on this continent, and the inhabitants of the West Indies, generally dwell in pure righteousness, I believe a small trade between us might be right. Under these considerations, when the thoughts of wholly declining the use of trading vessels, and of trying to hire a vessel to go in ballast have arisen in my mind, I have believed that the labors in Gospel love, yet bestowed in the cause of universal righteousness, are not arrived to that height.

"If the trade to the West Indies was no more than was consistent with pure wisdom, I believe the passage money would, for good reasons, be higher than it is now; and under deep exercise of mind, I have believed that I should not take the advantage of this great trade and small passage money; but as a testimony in favor of less trading, should pay more than is common for others to pay, if I go at this time."

The first-mentioned owner having read the paper, expressed a willingness to go with me to the other owner; and we going, the other owner read over the paper, and we had some solid conversation; under which, I felt my soul bowed in reverence before the Most High. At length one of them asked me, if I would go and see the vessel; but I had not clearness in my mind to go; but went to my lodgings and retired in private.

I was now under great exercise of mind; and my tears were poured out before the Lord, with inward cries that he would graciously help me under these trials.

In this case I believe my mind was resigned, but did not feel clearness to proceed; and my own weakness and the necessity of Divine instruction, were impressed upon me.

I was for a time as one who knew not what to do, and was tossed as in a tempest; under which affliction, the doctrine of Christ, "Take no thought for the morrow," arose livingly before me. I remembered that it was some days before they expected the vessel to sail, and was favored to get into a good degree of stillness; and having been nearly two days in town, I believed my obedience to my heavenly Father consisted in returning homeward. I went over amongst Friends on the Jersey shore, and tarried till the morning on which they had appointed to sail; and as I lay in bed the latter part of that night, my mind was comforted; and I felt what I esteemed a fresh confirmation, that it was the Lord's will I should pass through some further exercises near home.

So I went home, and still felt like a sojourner with my family, and in the fresh spring of pure love, had some labors in a private way amongst Friends, on a subject relating to Truth's testimony; under which I had frequently been exercised in heart for some years. I remember, as I walked on the road under this exercise, that passage in Ezekiel came fresh before me, "Whithersoever their faces were turned, thither they went"; and I was graciously helped to discharge my duty, in the fear and dread of the Almighty.

After a few weeks it pleased the Lord to visit me with a pleurisy; and after I had lain a few days, and felt the disorder very grievous, I was thoughtful how it might end.

I had, of late, through various exercises, been much weaned from the pleasant things of this life; and I now thought if it was the Lord's will to put an end to my labors, and graciously receive me into the arms of his mercy, death would be acceptable to me; but if it was his will further to refine me under affliction, and make me, in any degree, useful in his church, I desired not to die. I may with thankfulness say, that in this case I felt resignedness wrought in me, and had no inclination to send for a doctor; believing if it was the Lord's will, through outward means, to raise me up, some sympathizing Friends would be sent to minister to me; who were accordingly. But though I was carefully attended, yet the disorder was at times so heavy, that I had no thoughts of recovery. One night in particular, my bodily distress was great; my feet grew cold, and cold increased up my legs towards my body, and at that time I had no inclination to ask my nurse to apply anything warm to my feet, expecting my end was near. After I had lain nearly ten hours in this condition, I closed my eyes, thinking whether I might now be delivered out of the body; but in these awful moments my mind was livingly opened to behold the church, and strong engagements were begotten in me, for the everlasting well-being of my fellow-creatures; and I felt in the spring of pure love, that I might remain some time longer in the body, in filling up according to my measure, that which remains of the afflictions of Christ, and in laboring for the good of the church. After this I requested my nurse to apply warmth to my feet, and I revived. The next night feeling a weighty exercise of spirit, and having a solid Friend sitting up with me, I requested him to write what I said; which he did, as follows:—

"4th day of the first month, 1770, about five o'clock in the morning. I have seen in the light of the Lord, that the day is approaching when the man that is the most wise in human policy, shall be the greatest fool; and the arm that is mighty to support injustice, shall be broken to pieces. The enemies of righteousness shall make a terrible rattle, and shall mightily torment one another; for He that is omnipotent is rising up to judgment, and will plead the cause of the oppressed; and he commanded me to open the vision."

Near a week after this, feeling my mind livingly opened, I sent for a neighbor, who, at my request, wrote as follows: —

"The place of prayer is a precious habitation; for I now saw that the prayers of the saints were precious incense; and a trumpet was given me, that I might sound forth this language, that the children might hear it, and be invited to gather to this precious habitation, where the prayers of the saints, as precious incense, arise up before the throne of God and the Lamb — I saw this habitation to be safe; to be inwardly quiet, when there were great stirrings and commotions in the world.

"Prayer at this day, in pure resignation, is a precious place: the trumpet is sounded, the call goes forth to the church, that she gather to the place of pure inward prayer; and her habitation is safe."

CHAPTER XI

Preparing to visit Friends in England — Embarks at Chester, in company with Samuel Emlen, in a ship bound to London — His deep exercise, in observing the difficulties and hardships the common sailors are exposed to — Considerations on the dangers to which youths are exposed, in being trained to a sea-faring life; and its inconsistency with a pious education — Thoughts in a storm at sea; with many instructive contemplations on the voyage — Arrival at London.

HAVING been some time under a religious concern to prepare for crossing the seas, in order to visit Friends in the Northern parts of England, and more particularly in Yorkshire; after weighty consideration, I thought it expedient to inform Friends at our Monthly Meeting at Burlington of it; who having unity with me therein, gave me a certificate. I afterward communicated the same to our Quarterly Meeting, and they likewise certified their concurrence therewith. Some time after, at the General Spring Meeting of ministers and elders, I thought it my duty to acquaint them of the religious exercise which attended my mind; and they likewise signified their unity by a certificate, dated the 24th day of the third month, 1772, directed to Friends in Great Britain.

In the fourth month following, I thought the time was come for me to make some inquiry for a suitable conveyance; being apprehensive, that as my concern was principally toward the northern parts of England, it would be most proper to go in a vessel bound to Liverpool or Whitehaven. While I was at Philadelphia deliberating on this occasion, I was informed that my beloved friend Samuel Emlen, jr., intending to go to London, had taken passage for himself in the cabin of the ship called Mary and Elizabeth, of which James Sparks was master, and John Head of the city of Philadelphia, one of the owners; and I feeling a draft in my mind toward the steerage of the same ship, went first and opened to Samuel the feeling I had concerning it.

My beloved friend wept when I spoke to him, and appeared glad that I had thought of going in the vessel with him, though my prospect was toward the steerage; and he offering to go with me, we went on board, first into the cabin, a commodious room, and then into the steerage, where we sat down on a chest, the sailors being busy about us; the owner of the ship came and sat down with us.

Here my mind was turned toward Christ, the heavenly counsellor; and feeling at this time my own will subjected, my heart was contrite before him.

A motion was made by the owner to go and sit in the cabin, as a place more retired; but I felt easy to leave the ship, and made no agreement as to a passage in her; but told the owner, if I took a passage in the ship, I believed it would be in the steerage; but did not say much as to my exercise in that case.

After I went to my lodgings, and the case was a little known in town, a Friend laid before me the great inconvenience attending a passage in the steerage; which for a time appeared very discouraging to me.

I soon after went to bed, and my mind was under a deep exercise before the Lord, whose helping hand was manifested to me as I slept that night, and his love strengthened my heart. In the morning I went again with two Friends on board the vessel; and after a short time spent therein, I went with Samuel Emlen to the house of the owner; to whom in the hearing of Samuel, I opened my exercise in relation to a scruple I felt with regard to a passage in the cabin, which was in substance as follows: —

I told the owner that on the outside of that part of the ship where the cabin was, I observed sundry sorts of carved work and imagery; that in the cabin I observed some superfluity of workmanship of several sorts; and that according to the ways of men's reckoning, the sum of money to be paid for a passage in that apartment, had some relation to the expense of furnishing it to please the minds of such who give way to a conformity to this world; and that in this case, as in other cases, the moneys received from the passengers, are calculated to answer every expense relating to their passage, and amongst the rest of these superfluities: and that I felt a scruple with regard to paying my money to defray such expenses.

As my mind was now opened, I told the owner that I had at several times in my travels, seen great oppressions on this continent; at which my heart had been much affected, and brought into a feeling of the state of the sufferers. And having many times been engaged, in the fear and love of God, to labor with those under whom the oppressed have been borne down and afflicted, I have often perceived a desire prevalent to get riches and provide estates for children, to live comformably to customs, which stand in that spirit wherein men have regard to the honors of this world. In the pursuit of these things, I have seen many entangled in the spirit of oppression, and the exercise of my soul has been such, that I could not find peace in joining in anything which I saw was against that wisdom which is pure.

After this I agreed for a passage in the steerage; and hearing that Joseph White had a desire to see me, I felt the reviving of a desire to see him, and went to his house, and the next day home, where I tarried two nights: and then early in the morning, I parted with my family under a sense of the humbling hand of God upon me; and going to Philadelphia, had opportunity with several of my beloved friends, who appeared to be concerned for me, on account of the unpleasant situation of that part of the vessel, where I was likely to lodge.

In these opportunities my mind, through the mercies of the Lord, was kept low in an inward waiting for his help; and Friends having expressed their desire that I might have a place more convenient than the steerage, did not urge, but appeared disposed to leave me to the Lord.

Having staid two nights in Philadelphia, I went the next day to Darby Monthly Meeting; where, through the strength of Divine love, my heart was enlarged toward the youth then present; under which I was helped to labor in some tenderness of spirit. Then lodging at William Horne's, I, with one Friend, went to Chester; where meeting with Samuel Emlen, we went on board the 1st day of the fifth month, 1772: and as I sat alone on the deck, I felt a satisfactory evidence that my proceedings were not of my own will, but under the power of the cross of Christ.

7th day of the fifth month: have had rough weather mostly, since I came on board; and the passengers, James Reynolds, John Till Adams, Sarah Logan and her hired maid, and John Bispham, all sea-sick, more or less, at times; from which sickness, through the tender mercies of my heavenly Father, I have been preserved; my afflictions now being of another kind.

There appeared an openness in the minds of the master of the ship and of the cabin passengers toward me; we were often together on the deck, and sometimes in the cabin.

My mind, through the merciful help of the Lord, has been preserved in a good degree watchful, and inward; and I have this day, great cause to be thankful that I continue to feel quietness of mind.

As my lodging in the steerage, now nearly a week, has afforded me opportunities of seeing, hearing, and feeling, with respect to the life and spirit of many poor sailors; an inward exercise of soul has attended me, in regard to placing children and youth where they may be likely to be exampled and instructed in the pure fear of the Lord. Being much amongst the seamen, I have from a motion of love, several times taken opportunities with one of them at a time alone; and in a free conversation, labored to turn their minds toward the fear of the Lord. This day we had a meeting in the cabin, where my heart was contrited under a feeling of Divine love.

Concerning lads being trained up as seamen; I believe a communication by sea from one part of the world to other parts of it is at times consistent with the will of our heavenly Father; and to educate some youth in the practice of sailing, I believe may be right. But how lamentable is the present corruption of the world! how impure are the channels through which trade has a conveyance! how great is the danger to which poor lads are exposed, when placed on shipboard to learn the art of sailing!

Five lads training up for the seas were now on board of this ship; two of them brought up amongst our Society, and one has a right amongst Friends, by name James Nayler, to whose father, James Nayler, mentioned in Sewel's History appears to have been uncle.

I often feel a tenderness of heart toward these poor lads; and at times look at them as though they were my children according to the flesh.

O that all may take heed and beware of covetousness! O that all may learn of Christ, who was meek and low of heart! then in faithfully following him, he will teach us to be content with food and raiment, without respect to the customs or honors of this world.

Men thus redeemed, will feel a tender concern for their fellow-creatures, and a desire that those in the lowest stations may be assisted and encouraged; and where owners of ships attain to the perfect law of liberty, and are doers of the word, these will be blessed in their deeds.

A ship at sea commonly sails all night, and the seamen take their watches four hours at a time.

Rising to work in the night, is not commonly pleasant in any case; but in dark rainy nights it is very disagreeable, even though each man were furnished with all conveniences. But if men must go out at midnight to help manage the ship in the rain, and having small room to sleep and lay their garments in, are often beset to furnish themselves for the watch; their garments or something relating to their business being wanting, and not easily found; when from the urgency occasioned by high winds, they are hastened and called up suddenly; here is a trial of patience on the poor sailors, and the poor lads their companions.

If after they have been on deck several hours in the night, they come down into the steerage soaking wet, and are so closely stowed that proper convenience for change of garment is not easily come at, but for want of proper room their wet garments thrown in heaps, and sometimes, through much crowding, are trodden under foot, in going to their lodgings and getting out of them, and great difficulty at times, each one to find his own; here are trials on the poor sailors.

As I have been with them in my lodge, my heart has often yearned for them; and tender desires been raised in me, that owners and masters of vessels may dwell in the love of God, and therein act uprightly; and by seeking less for gain, and looking carefully to their ways, may earnestly labor to remove all cause of provocation from the poor seamen, either to fret or use excess of strong drink; for indeed the poor creatures at times, in the wet and cold, seem to apply to strong drink to supply the want of other conveniences.

Great reformation in the world is wanting, and the necessity of it amongst those who do business on the great waters, has at this time been abundantly opened before me.

The 8th day of the fifth month. This morning the clouds gathered, the wind blew strong from the south-eastward, and before noon increased to a degree that made sailing appear dangerous. The seamen then bound up some of their sails and took down some; and the storm increasing, they put the dead light, so called, into the cabin windows, and lighted a lamp as at night.

The wind now blew vehemently, and the sea wrought to such a degree, that an awful seriousness prevailed in the cabin, in which I spent, I believe, about seventeen hours; for I believed the poor wet toiling seamen had need of all the room in the crowded steerage, and the cabin passengers had given me frequent invitations.

They ceased now from sailing, and put the vessel in the posture called lying-to.

My mind during this tempest, through the gracious assistance of the Lord, was preserved in a good degree of resignation; and I felt at times a few words in his love to my ship-mates, in regard to the all-sufficiency of Him who formed the great deep, and whose care is so extensive that a sparrow falls not without his notice. Thus in a tender frame of mind I spoke to them of the necessity of our yielding, in true obedience, to the instructions of our heavenly Father, who sometimes through adversities intendeth our refinement.

About eleven o'clock at night I went out on the deck, when the sea wrought exceedingly, and the high foaming waves, all around, had in some sort the appearance of fire; but did not give much, if any light. The sailor then at the helm said he lately saw a corposant at the head of the mast.

About this time I observed the master of the ship ordered the carpenter to keep on deck; and though he said little, I apprehended his care was, that the carpenter with his axe might be in readiness, in case of any extremity.

Soon after this, the vehemency of the wind abated; and before morning they again put the ship under sail.

The 10th day of the month and first of the week, being fine weather, we had a meeting in the cabin, at which most of the seamen were present; and to me it was a strengthening time.

The 13th day of the month. As I continue to lodge in the steerage, I feel an openness this morning to express something further of the state of my mind, in respect to lads bound apprentice to learn the art of sailing. As I believe sailing is of some use in the world, a labor of soul attends me, that the pure counsel of Truth may be humbly waited for, in this case, by all concerned in the business of the seas.

A pious father, whose mind is exercised for the everlasting welfare of his child, may not, with a peaceable mind, place him out to an employment amongst a people whose common course of life is manifestly corrupt and profane. So great is the present defect amongst seafaring men, in regard to piety and virtue, and through an abundant traffic, and many ships of war, so many people are employed on the sea, that the subject of placing lads to this employment appears very weighty.

Profane examples are very corrupting and very forcible. As my mind, day after day, and night after night, has been affected with a sympathizing tenderness toward poor children put to the employment of sailors, I have sometimes had weighty conversation with the sailors in the steerage, who were mostly respectful to me, and more so the longer I was with them. They mostly appeared to take kindly what I said to them; but their minds appeared to be so deeply impressed with the almost universal depravity amongst sailors, that the poor creatures, in their answers to me on this subject, revived in my remembrance that of the degenerate Jews a little before the captivity, as repeated by Jeremiah the prophet, "There is no hope."

Under this exercise a sense of the desire of outward gain prevailing amongst us, hath felt grievous; and a strong call to the professed followers of Christ, hath been raised in me, that all may take heed, lest through loving this present world, they be found in a continued neglect of duty, with respect to a faithful labor for a reformation.

Silence, as to every motion proceeding from the love of

money, and an humble waiting upon God to know his will concerning us, appear necessary: he alone is able to strengthen us to dig deep, to remove all which lies between us and the safe foundation, and so to direct us in our outward employments, that pure universal love may shine forth in our proceedings.

Desires arising from the Spirit of Truth, are pure desires; and when a mind, divinely opened toward a young generation, is made sensible of corrupting examples, powerfully working and extensively spreading amongst them, how moving is the prospect!

There is a great trade to the coast of Africa for slaves; of which I heard frequent conversation among the sailors!

A great trade in that which is raised and prepared through grievous oppression!

A great trade in superfluity of workmanship formed to please the pride and vanity of people's minds!

Great and extensive is that depravity which prevails amongst the poor sailors!

When I remember that saying of the Most High, through his prophet, "This people have I formed for myself; they shall show forth my praise," and think of placing children amongst them, to learn the practice of sailing, the consistency of it with a pious education, seems to me like that mentioned by the prophet, "There is no answer from God."

In a world of dangers and difficulties, like a desolate thorny wilderness, how precious, how comfortable, how safe, are the leadings of Christ, the good Shepherd; who said, "I know my sheep, and am known of mine."

The 16th day of the month. Wind for several days past often high, what the sailors call squally, rough sea and frequent rains. This last night was a very trying one to the poor seamen; the water, during the chief part of it, running over the main deck, and sometimes breaking waves came on the quarter-deck. The latter part of the night, as I lay in bed, my mind was humbled under the power of Divine love; and resignedness to the great Creator of the earth and the seas, was renewedly wrought in me, whose fatherly care over his children felt precious to my soul. Desires were now renewed in me, to embrace every opportunity of being inwardly acquainted with the hardships and difficulties of my fellow-creatures, and to labor in his love for the spreading of pure universal righteousness on the earth. The opportunities were frequent of hearing conversation amongst the sailors, in respect to the voyages to Africa, the manner of bringing the deeply oppressed slaves into our islands, the thought of their condition on board the vessels, frequently in chains and fetters, with hearts loaded with grief, under the apprehensions of miserable slavery; and my mind was frequently opened to meditate on these things.

On the 17th day of the month and first of the week, we had a meeting in the cabin; to which the seamen generally came. My spirit was contrite before the Lord; whose love at this time affected my heart.

This afternoon I felt a tender sympathy of soul with my poor wife and family left behind; in which state my heart was enlarged in desires that they may walk in that humble obedience wherein the everlasting Father may be their guide and support, through all the difficulties in this world; and a sense of that gracious assistance, through which my mind hath been strengthened to take up the cross and leave them, to travel in the love of Truth, begot thankfulness in my heart to our great Helper.

On the 24th day of the month and first of the week, a clear pleasant morning; and as I sat on deck, I felt a reviving in my nature; which, through much rainy weather and high winds, being shut up in a close unhealthy air, was weakened.

Several nights of late I felt breathing so difficult, that a little after the rising of the second watch, which is about midnight, I got up, and stood, I believe, nearly an hour with my face near the hatchway, to get the fresh air at a small vacancy under the hatch door, which is commonly shut down, partly to keep out rain, and sometimes to keep the breaking waves from dashing into the steerage.

I may, with thankfulness to the Father of mercies, acknowledge that in my present weak state, my mind hath been supported to bear the affliction with patience; and I have looked at the present dispensation as a kindness from the great Father of mankind, who, in this my floating pilgrimage, is in some degree bringing me to feel what many thousands of my fellow-creatures often suffer in a greater degree.

My appetite failing, the trial has been the heavier; and I have felt tender breathings in my soul after God, the fountain of comfort, whose inward help has supplied, at times, the want of outward convenience: and strong desires have attended me, that his family, who are acquainted with the movings of his Holy Spirit, may be so redeemed from the love of money, and from that spirit in which men seek honor one of another, that in all business, by sea or land, we may constantly keep in view the coming of his kingdom on earth, as it is in heaven; and by faithfully following this safe guide, show forth examples, tending to lead out of those things under which the creation groans!

This day we had a meeting in the cabin; in which I was favored in some degree to experience the fulfilling of that saying of the prophet, "The Lord hath been a strength to the poor, a strength to the needy in their distress"; for which my heart is bowed in thankfulness before him.

The 28th day of the month: wet weather of late, with small winds inclining to calms; our seamen cast a lead, I suppose about one hundred fathoms, but found no bottom: foggy weather this morning.

Through the kindness of the great Preserver of men, my mind remains quiet; and a degree of exercise from day to day attends me, that the pure peaceable government of Christ may spread and prevail amongst mankind.

The leading on of a young generation, in that pure way, in which the wisdom of this world hath no place; where parents and tutors, humbly waiting for the heavenly Counsellor, may example them in the Truth as it is in Jesus, has for several days been the exercise of my mind. O how safe, how quiet is that state, where the soul stands in pure obedience to the voice of Christ, and a watchful care is maintained, not to follow the voice of the stranger!

Here, Christ is felt to be our Shepherd; and under his leading, people are brought to a stability; and where he doth not lead forward, we are bound in the bonds of pure love, to stand still and wait upon him. In the love of money, and in the wisdom of this world, business is proposed, then the urgency of affairs pushes forward; nor can the mind in this state discern the good and perfect will of God concerning us.

The love of God is manifested in graciously calling us to come out of that which stands in confusion; but if we bow not in the name of Jesus; if we give not up those prospects of gain, which in the wisdom of this world are open before us, but say in our hearts, I must needs go on; and in going on, I hope to keep as near to the purity of Truth as the business before me will admit of; here the mind remains entangled, and the shining of the light of life into the soul is obstructed.

This query opens in my mind in the love of Christ; where shall a pious father place his son apprentice, to be instructed in the practice of crossing the seas; and have faith to believe, that Christ our holy Shepherd leads him to place his son there?

Surely the Lord calls to mourning and deep humiliation, that in his fear we may be instructed, and led safely on through the great difficulties and perplexities of the present age.

In an entire subjection of our wills, the Lord graciously opens a way for his people, where all their wants are bounded by his wisdom; and here we experience the substance of what Moses the prophet figured out in the water of separation as a purification from sin.

Esau is mentioned as a child red all over, like a hairy garment: in Esau is represented the natural will of man. In preparing the water of separation, a red heifer without blemish, on which there had been no yoke, was to be slain, and her blood sprinkled by the priest seven times toward the tabernacle of the congregation. Then her skin, her flesh, and all pertaining to her, were to be burnt without the camp; and of her ashes the water was prepared. Thus the crucifying of the old man, or natural will, is represented; and hence comes a separation from that carnal mind, which is death.

"He who toucheth the dead body of a man, and purifieth not himself with the water of separation, he defileth the tabernacle of the Lord; he is unclean."

If any through the love of gain, go forth into business, wherein they dwell as amongst the tombs, and touch the bodies of those who are dead: if these, through the infinite love of God, feel the power of the cross of Christ to crucify them to the world, and therein learn humbly to follow the Divine leader; here is the judgment of this world — here the prince of this world is cast out.

The water of separation is felt; and though we have been amongst the slain, and through the desire of gain have touched the dead body of a man; yet in the purifying love of Christ, we are washed in the water of separation, are brought off from that business, from that gain, and from that fellowship, which are not agreeable to his holy will. I have felt a renewed confirmation in the time of this voyage, that the Lord, in his infinite love, is calling to his visited children, so to give up all outward possessions and means of getting treasures, that his Holy Spirit may have free course in their hearts, and direct them in all their proceedings.

To feel the substance pointed at in this figure, man must know death, as to his own will.

"No man can see God, and live." This was spoken by the Almighty to Moses the prophet; and opened by our blessed Redeemer.

As death comes on our own wills, and a new life is formed in us, the heart is purified and prepared to understand clearly. "Blessed are the pure in heart, for they shall see God." In purity of heart, the mind is Divinely opened to behold the nature of universal righteousness, or the righteousness of the kingdom of God. "No man hath seen the Father, save that he is of God; he hath seen the Father."

The natural mind is active about the things of this life; and in this natural activity, business is proposed, and there is a will in us to go forward in it. And as long as this natural will remains unsubjected, so long there remains an obstruction against the clearness of Divine light operating in us; but when we love God with all our heart, and with all our strength, then in this love we love our neighbors as ourselves; and a tenderness of heart is felt toward all people for whom Christ died, even such who as to outward circumstances may be to us as the Jews were to the Samaritans. "Who is my neighbor?" See this question answered by our Saviour, Luke x. 30.

In this love we can say, that Jesus is the Lord; and the reformation in our souls is manifested in a full reformation of our lives, wherein all things are new, and all things are of God; 2 Cor. v. 18, in this the desire of gain is subjected.

When employment is honestly followed in the light of Truth; and people become diligent in business, "fervent in spirit, serving the Lord," the name is opened; "This is the name by which he shall be called, The Lord our Righteousness." Oh, how precious is this name! It is like ointment poured out. The chaste virgins are in love with the Redeemer; and for promoting his peaceable kingdom in the world, are content to endure hardness like good soldiers; and are so separated in spirit from the desire of riches, that in their employments, they become extensively careful to give no offence, either to Jews, or heathen, or the church of Christ.

On the 31st day of the month, and first of the week, we had a meeting in the cabin, with nearly all the ship's company; the whole being nearly thirty. In this meeting, the Lord, in mercy, favored us with the extendings of his love.

The 2nd day of the sixth month. Last evening the seamen found bottom at about seventy fathoms.

This morning there was a fair wind, and it was pleasant: as I sat on deck my heart was overcome with the love of Christ, and melted into contrition before him: and in this state, the prospect of that work, to which I have felt my mind drawn when in my native land, being in some degree opened before me, I felt like a little child; and my cries were put up to my heavenly Father for preservation, that in an humble dependence on him, my soul may be strengthened in his love, and kept inwardly waiting for his counsel.

This afternoon we saw that part of England called the Lizard.

Some dunghill fowls yet remained of those the passengers took for their sea-stores: I believe about fourteen perished in the storms at sea, by the waves breaking over the quarter-deck; and a considerable number with sickness, at different times. I observed the cocks crow coming down the Delaware, and while we were near the land; but afterward, I think I did not hear one of them crow till we came near the land in England, when they again crowed a few times.

In observing their dull appearance at sea, and the pining sickness of some of them, I often remembered the fountain of Goodness, who gave being to all creatures, and whose love extends even to caring for the sparrows; and I believe, where the love of God is verily perfected, and the true spirit of government watchfully attended to, a tenderness toward all creatures made subject to us will be experienced; and a care felt, that we do not lessen that sweetness of life, in the animal creation, which the great Creator intends for them under our government.

The 4th day of the month. Wet weather, with high winds, and so dark that we could see but a little way. I perceived our seamen were apprehensive of missing the channel: which I understood was narrow. In a while it grew lighter; and they saw the land, and knew where we were. Thus the Father of mercies was pleased to try us with the sight of dangers; and then graciously from time to time deliver from them; sparing our lives, that in humility and reverence, we may walk before him, and put our trust in him.

About noon a pilot came off from Dover; where my beloved friend Samuel Emlen went on shore, and thence to London, about seventy-two miles by land; but I felt easy in staying in the ship.

The 7th day of the month, and first of the week. A clear morning; we lay at anchor for the tide, and had a parting meeting with the ship's company; in which my heart was enlarged in a fervent concern for them, that they may come to experience salvation through Christ. Had a head wind up the Thames; sometimes lay at anchor, and saw many ships passing, and some at anchor near; and had large opportunity of feeling the spirit in which the poor bewildered sailors too generally live. That lamentable degeneracy, which so much prevails among the people employed on the seas, so affected my heart, that I may not easily convey to another the feeling I have had.

The present state of a sea-faring life in general, appears so opposite to a pious education; so full of corruption, and extreme alienation from God; so full of examples, the most dangerous to young people, that in looking toward a young generation, I feel a care for them, that they may have an education different from the present education of lads at sea: and that all of us, who are acquainted with the pure Gospel spirit, may lay this case to heart, may remember the lamentable corruptions which attend the conveyance of merchandize across the seas, and so abide in the love of Christ, that being delivered from the love of money, from the entangling expenses of a curious, delicate, and luxurious life, we may learn contentment with a little; and promote the sea-faring life no further, than that spirit, which leads into all truth, attends us in our proceedings.

CHAPTER XII

Attends the Yearly Meeting in London — Proceeds toward Yorkshire, visiting several Quarterly and other meetings in the counties of Hertford, Warwick, Oxford, Nottingham, York, and Westmoreland; and thence again into Yorkshire, and to the city of York — Some instructive thoughts and observations — Letters on divers subjects — Hears of the decease of William Hunt; some account of him — Sickness at York; and death there.

On the 8th day of the sixth month, 1772, we landed at London; and I went straightway to the Yearly Meeting of ministers and elders, which had been gathered, I suppose, about half an hour.

In this meeting, my mind was humbly contrite: in the afternoon, the meeting of business opened, which by adjournments held near a week. In these meetings, I often felt a living concern for the establishment of Friends in the pure life of Truth; and my heart was enlarged in the meeting of ministers, meeting of business, and in several meetings for public worship; and I felt my mind united in true love to the faithful laborers now gathered at this Yearly Meeting.

On the 15th day of the month I left London, and went to a Quarterly Meeting at Hertford.

The 1st day of the seventh month. I have been at Quarterly Meetings at Sherrington, Northampton, Banbury, and Shipton, and had sundry meetings between. My mind has been bowed under a sense of Divine goodness manifested amongst us; my heart being often enlarged in true love, both amongst ministers and elders, and in public meetings; and through the Lord's goodness, I believe it has been a fresh visitation to many, in particular to the youth.

The 17th day of the month. Was this day at Birmingham: have been at meetings at Coventry, Warwick, and Oxfordshire, and sundry other places; I have felt the humbling hand of the Lord upon me, and through his tender mercies find peace in the labors I have gone through.

The 26th day of the month. I have continued travelling northward visiting meetings: was this day at Nottingham; which, in the forenoon especially, was through Divine love a heart-tendering season: next day had a meeting with Friends' children and some Friends; this, through the strengthening arm of the Lord, was a time to be thankfully remembered.

The 2d day of the eighth month, and first of the week, was this day at Sheffield, a large inland town: I have been at sundry meetings last week, and feel inward thankfulness for that Divine support which hath been graciously extended to me.

The 9th day of the month, and first of the week, was at Rushworth: have lately passed through some painful labor; but I have been comforted, under a sense of that Divine visitation, which I feel extended toward many young people.

The 16th day of the month, the first of the week, was at Settle: it has of late been a time of inward poverty; under which, my mind has been preserved in a watchful tender state, feeling for the mind of the holy Leader, and find peace in the labors I have passed through.

On inquiry, in many places, I find the price of rye about five shillings, and wheat about eight shillings, per bushel; oatmeal twelve shillings for a hundred and twenty pounds; mutton from three-pence to five-pence per pound; bacon, from seven-pence to nine-pence; cheese, from four-pence to six-pence; butter, from eight-pence to ten-pence; house-rent, for a poor man, from twenty-five shillings to forty shillings per year, to be paid weekly; wood for fire, very scarce and dear; coal, in some places, two shillings and six-pence per hundred weight; but near the pits, not a quarter so much. O, may the wealthy consider the poor!

The wages of laboring men in several counties toward London, are ten-pence per day in common business, the employer finds small-beer, and the laborer finds his own food; but in harvest, and hay time, wages are about one shilling per day, and the laborer has all his diet. In some parts of the north of England, poor laboring men have their food where they work, and appear, in common, to do rather better than nearer London. Industrious women, who spin in the factories, get some four-pence, some five-pence, and so on to six, seven, eight, nine, or ten-pence per day, and find their own house-room and diet. Great numbers of poor people live chiefly on bread and water in the southern parts of England, and some in the northern parts; and there are many poor children not even taught to read. May those who have plenty lay these things to heart!

Stage-coaches frequently go upwards of an hundred miles in twenty-four hours; and I have heard Friends say, in several places, that it is common for horses to be killed with hard driving, and many others are driven until they grow blind.

Post-boys pursue their business, each one to his stage, all night through the winter: some boys who ride long stages, suffer greatly during winter nights; and at several places I have heard of their being frozen to death. So great is the hurry in the spirit of this world, that in aiming to do business quick and to gain wealth, the creation at this day doth loudly groan!

As my journey has been without a horse, I have had several offers of being assisted on my way in stage-coaches; but have not been in them; nor have I had freedom to send letters by these posts, in the present way of their riding; the stages being so fixed, and one boy dependent on another as to time, that they commonly go upward of one hundred miles in twenty-four hours; and in the cold long winter nights, the poor boys suffer much.

I heard in America of the way of these posts; and cautioned Friends in the General Meeting of ministers and elders of Philadelphia, and in the Yearly Meeting of ministers and elders at London, not to send letters to me on any common occasion by post. And though on this account I may be likely to hear more seldom from my family left behind, yet for righteousness sake, I am through Divine favor made content.

I have felt great distress of mind, since I came on this island, on account of the members of our Society being mixed with the world, in various sorts of business and traffic, carried on in impure channels. Great is the trade of Africa for slaves! ° and in loading these ships, abundance of people are employed in the factories; amongst whom are many of our Society. Friends in early times refused on a religious principle, to make or trade in superfluities, of which we have many large testimonies on record: but for want of faithfulness some gave way, even some whose examples were of note in our Society; and from thence others took more liberty. Members of our Society worked in superfluities, and bought and sold them; and thus dimness of sight came over many. At length, Friends got into the use of some superfluities in dress, and in the furniture of their houses; and this has spread from less to more, until superfluity of some kinds is common amongst us.

In this declining state, many look at the example one of another, and too much neglect the pure feeling of Truth. Of late years, a deep exercise has attended my mind, that Friends may dig deep, may carefully cast forth the loose matter, and get down to the Rock, the sure foundation, and there hearken to that Divine voice which gives a clear and certain sound. I have felt in that which doth not deceive, that if Friends who have known the Truth, keep in that tenderness of heart, where all views of outward gain are given up, and their trust is only on the Lord, he will graciously lead some to be patterns of deep self-denial in things relating to trade and handicraft labor; and that some who have plenty of the treasures of this world, will set an example of a plain frugal life, and pay wages to such whom they may hire, more liberally than is now customary in some places.

The 23d day of the month; was this day at Preston-Patrick, and had a comfortable meeting. I have several times been entertained at the houses of Friends, who had sundry things about them which had the appearance of outward greatness; and as I have kept inward, way has opened for conversation with such in private, in which Divine goodness has favored us together with heart-tendering times.

The 26th day of the month. Being now at George Crosfields, in the county of Westmoreland, I feel a concern to commit to writing that which to me hath been a case uncommon.

In a time of sickness with the pleurisy, a little upward of two years and a half ago, I was brought so near the gates of death, that I forgot my name: being then desirous to know who I was, I saw a mass of matter of a dull gloomy color, between the south and the east; and was informed, that this mass was human beings in as great misery as they could be, and live; and that I was mixed in with them, and that henceforth I might not consider myself as a distinct or separate being. In this state I remained several hours. I then heard a soft melodious voice, more pure and harmonious than any I had heard before. I believed it was the voice of an angel, who spake to the other angels, and the words were these, *John Woolman is dead.* I soon remembered that I once was John Woolman; and being assured that I was alive in the body, I greatly wondered what that heavenly voice could mean.

I believed beyond doubting that it was the voice of an holy angel; but as yet it was a mystery to me.

I was then carried in spirit to the mines, where poor oppressed people were digging rich treasures for those called Christians; and I heard them blaspheme the name of Christ, at which I was grieved; for his name to me was precious.

Then I was informed, that these heathens were told, that those who oppressed them were the followers of Christ; and they said amongst themselves, If Christ directed them to use us in this sort, then Christ is a cruel tyrant.

All this time the song of the angel remained a mystery; and in the morning, my dear wife and some others coming to my bed-side, I asked them if they knew who I was; and they telling me I was John Woolman, thought I was light-headed: for I told them not what the angel said, nor was I disposed to talk much to any one; but was very desirous to get so deep, that I might understand this mystery.

My tongue was often so dry, that I could not speak till I had moved it about and gathered some moisture, and as I lay still for a time, at length I felt Divine power prepare my mouth that I could speak; and then I said, "I am crucified with Christ, nevertheless I live; yet not I, but Christ liveth in me: and the life which I now live in the flesh, I live by the faith of the Son of God, who loved me, and gave himself for me."

Then the mystery was opened; and I perceived there was joy in heaven over a sinner who had repented; and that that language (John Woolman is dead) meant no more than the death of my own will.

Soon after this I coughed, and raised much bloody matter; which I had not done during this vision; and now my natural understanding returned as before. Here I saw, that people getting silver vessels to set off their tables at entertainments, was often stained with worldly glory; and that in the present state of things, I should take heed how I fed myself out of silver vessels.

Soon after my recovery, going to our Monthly Meeting, I dined at a Friend's house where drink was brought in silver vessels, and not in any other; and wanting some drink, I told him my case with weeping; and he ordered some drink for me in another vessel.

The like I afterwards went through in several Friends' houses in America, and have also in England, since I came here: and have cause, with humble reverence, to acknowledge the loving-kindness of my heavenly Father, who hath preserved me in such a tender frame of mind, that none, I believe, have ever been offended at what I have said on that occasion.

After this sickness, I spake not in public meetings for worship for nearly one year: but my mind was very often in company with the oppressed slaves, as I sat in meetings: and though under this dispensation, I was shut up from speaking, yet the spring of the Gospel ministry was many times livingly opened in me; and the Divine gift operated by abundance of weeping, in feeling the oppression of this people. It being long since I passed through this dispensation, and the matter remaining fresh and livingly in my mind, I believe it safest for me to commit it to writing.

The 30th day of the month. This morning I wrote a letter, in substance as follows: —

"Beloved friend,

"My mind is often affected as I pass along, under a sense of the state of many poor people, who sit under that sort of ministry which requires much outward labor to support it; and the loving-kindness of our heavenly Father, in opening a pure Gospel ministry in this nation, hath often raised thankfulness in my heart to him. I often remember the conflicts of the faithful under persecution, and now look at the free exercise of the pure gift, uninterrupted by outward laws, as a trust committed to us, which requires our deepest gratitude, and most careful attention. I feel a tender concern, that the work of reformation, so prosperously carried on in this land within a few ages past, may go forward and spread amongst the nation; and may not go backward, through dust gathering on our garments, who have been called to a work so great and so precious.

"Last evening I had a little opportunity at thy house with some of thy family in thy absence, in which I rejoiced; and feeling a sweetness on my mind toward thee, I now endeavor to open a little of the feeling I had there.

"I have heard that in these parts, you had, at certain seasons meetings of conference, in relation to Friends living up to our principles, in which several meetings unite in one: with which I feel unity. I have in some measure, felt Truth lead that way amongst Friends in America; and have found, my dear friend, that in these labors, all superfluities in our own living are against us. I feel that pure love toward thee, in which there is freedom.

"I look at that precious gift bestowed on thee, with awfulness before Him who gave it; and feel a care, that we may be so separated to the Gospel of Christ, that those things which proceed from the spirit of this world, may have no place amongst us.

"Thy friend,

"JOHN WOOLMAN."

I rested a few days, in body and mind, with our friend Jane Crosfield, who was once in America: was on the sixth day of the week, at Kendal in Westmoreland; and at Grayrig meeting the 30th day of the month, and first of the week.

I have known poverty of late, and been graciously supported to keep in the patience; and am thankful, under a sense of the goodness of the Lord toward those that are of a contrite spirit.

The 6th day of the ninth month and first of the week; was this day at Counterside, a large meeting-house and very full: and through the opening of pure love, it was a strengthening time to me, and I believe to many more.

The 13th day of the month. Was this day at Richmond, a small meeting; but the town's people coming in, the house was crowded: it was a time of heavy labor; and I believe was a profitable meeting.

At this place I heard that my kinsman William Hunt from North Carolina, who was on a religious visit to Friends in England, departed this life on the 9th day of the ninth month instant, of the smallpox, at Newcastle. He appeared in the ministry when a youth; and his labors therein were of good savor. He travelled much in that work in America. I once heard him say in public testimony, that his concern was, in that visit, to be devoted to the service of Christ so fully, that he might not spend one minute in pleasing himself; which words, joined with his example, were a means of stirring up the pure mind in me.

Having of late travelled often in wet weather, through narrow streets in towns and villages, where there were dirtiness under foot, and the scent arising from that filth, which more or less infects the air of all thickly settled towns; and being but weakly, I have felt distress both in body and mind, with that which is impure.

In these journeys I have been where much cloth has been dyed; and sundry times walked over ground, where much of the dye stuffs have drained away. I have felt a longing in my mind, that people might come into cleanness of spirit, cleanness of person, and cleanness about their houses and garments.

Some who are great carry delicacy to a great height themselves, and yet real cleanliness is not generally promoted. Dyes being invented partly to please the eye, and partly to hide dirt, I have felt in this weak state, travelling in dirtiness and affected with unwholesome scents, a strong desire that the practice of dyeing cloth to hide dirt may be more fully considered.

To hide dirt in our garments, appears opposite to real cleanliness.

To wash garments and keep them sweet, appears cleanly.

Through giving way to hiding dirt in our garments, a spirit which would cover that which is disagreeable is strengthened.

Real cleanness becometh a holy people : but hiding that which is not clean by coloring our garments, appears contrary to the sweetness of sincerity.

Through some sorts of dyes, cloth is less useful ; and if the value of dye-stuffs, the expense of dyeing, and the damage done to cloth were all added together, and that expense applied to keep all sweet and clean, how much more cleanly would people be.

On this visit to England I have felt some instructions sealed on my mind, which I am concerned to leave in writing, for the use of such who are called to the station of a minister of Christ.

Christ being the Prince of peace, and we being no more than ministers, I find it necessary for us, not only to feel a concern in our first going forth, but to experience the renewing thereof, in the appointment of meetings.

I felt a concern in America, to prepare for this voyage ; and being through the mercy of God brought safely here, my heart was like a vessel that wanted vent, and for several weeks at first, when my mouth was opened in meetings, it often felt like the raising of a gate in a water course, where a weight of water lay upon it ; and in these labors there appeared a fresh visitation to many, especially the youth ; but sometimes after this, I felt empty and poor, and yet felt a necessity to appoint meetings.

In this state I was exercised to abide in the pure life of Truth, and in all my labors to watch diligently against the motions of self in my own mind.

I have frequently felt a necessity to stand up, when the spring of the ministry was low, and to speak from the necessity, in that which subjecteth the will of the creature; and herein I was united with the suffering seed, and found inward sweetness in these mortifying labors.

As I have been preserved in a watchful attention to the Divine Leader under these dispensations, enlargement at times hath followed, and the power of Truth hath risen higher in some meetings, than I ever knew it before through me.

Thus I have been more and more instructed as to the necessity of depending, not upon a concern which I felt in America, to come on a visit to England; but upon the fresh instructions of Christ the Prince of peace, from day to day.

Now of late, I felt a stop in the appointment of meetings, not wholly but in part; and I do not feel liberty to appoint them so quickly one after another as I have heretofore.

The work of the ministry being a work of Divine love, I feel that the openings thereof are to be waited for in all our appointments.

O how deep is Divine wisdom! Christ puts forth his ministers, and goeth before them; and oh how great is the danger of departing from the pure feeling of that which leadeth safely!

Christ knoweth the state of the people, and in the pure feeling of the Gospel ministry, their states are opened to his servants.

Christ knoweth when the fruit-bearing branches themselves have need of purging.

Oh that these lessons may be remembered by me! and that all who appoint meetings, may proceed in the pure feeling of duty.

I have sometimes felt a necessity to stand up, but that spirit which is of the world hath so much prevailed in many, and the pure life of Truth has been so pressed down, that I have gone forward, not as one travelling in a road cast up and well prepared, but as a man walking through a miry place, in which are stones here and there, safe to step on; but so situated that one step being taken, time is necessary to see where to step next.

I find that in the pure obedience, the mind learns contentment in appearing weak and foolish to that wisdom which is of the world; and in these lowly labors, they who stand in a low place, rightly exercised under the cross, will find nourishment.

The gift is pure, and while the eye is single in attending thereto, the understanding is preserved clear; self is kept out; and we rejoice in filling up that which remains of the afflictions of Christ, for his body's sake, which is the church.

The natural man loveth eloquence, and many love to hear eloquent orations; and if there is not a careful attention to the gift, men who have once labored in the pure Gospel ministry, growing weary of suffering, and ashamed of appearing weak, may kindle a fire, compass themselves about with sparks and walk in the light, not of Christ who is under suffering, but of that fire, which they going from the gift have kindled. And that in hearers which is gone from the meek suffering state into the worldly wisdom, may be warmed with this fire, and speak highly of these labors. That which is of God gathers to God; and that which is of the world is owned by the world.

In this journey a labor hath attended my mind, that the ministers amongst us may be preserved in the meek, feeling life of Truth, where we may have no desire, but to follow Christ and be with him; that is when he under suffering we may suffer with him; and never desire to rise up in dominion, but as he by the virtue of his own spirit may raise us.

A few days after writing these considerations, our dear friend in the course of his religious visits came to the city of York, and attended most of the sittings of the Quarterly Meeting there; but before it was over, was taken ill of the smallpox. Our friend Thomas Priestman and others who attended him, preserved the following minutes of his expressions in the time of his sickness, and of his decease.

First-day, the 27th of the ninth month, 1772. His disorder appeared to be the smallpox: being asked to have a doctor's advice, he signified he had not freedom or liberty in his mind so to do, standing wholly resigned to his will who gave him life, and whose power he had witnessed to raise and heal him in sickness before, when he seemed nigh unto death; and if he was to wind up now, he was perfectly resigned, having no will either to live or die, and did not choose any should be sent for to him. But a young man an apothecary coming of his own accord the next day, and desiring to do something for him, he said he found a freedom to confer with him and the other Friend, about him, and if anything should be proposed, as to medicines that did not come through defiled channels or oppressive hands, he should be willing to consider and take it, so far as he found freedom.

Second-day. He said he felt the disorder to affect his head, so that he could think little, and but as a child; and desired if his understanding should be more affected, to have nothing given him that those about him knew he had a testimony against.

Third-day he uttered the following prayer. "O, Lord my God, the amazing horrors of darkness were gathered around me and covered me all over, and I saw no way to go forth. I felt the depth and extent of the misery of my fellow-creatures separated from the Divine harmony, and it was heavier than I could bear, and I was crushed down under it. I lifted up my hand, I stretched out my arm, but there was none to help me. I looked round about and was amazed. In the depth of misery, O Lord! I remembered that thou are omnipotent, that I had called thee Father, and I felt that I loved thee, and I was made quiet in thy will, and I waited for deliverance from thee. Thou hadst pity upon me when no man could help me. I saw that meekness under suffering was showed to us in the most affecting example of thy Son, and thou taught me to follow him, and I said, thy will, O Father, be done."

Fourth-day morning, being asked how he felt himself, he meekly answered, I don't know that I have slept this night. I feel the disorder making its progress, but my mind is mercifully preserved in stillness and peace. — Some time after he said he was sensible the pains of death must be hard to bear, but if he escaped them now, he must some time pass through them, and he did not know that he could be better prepared, but had no will in it. He said he had settled his outward affairs to his mind, and had taken leave of his wife and family as never to return, leaving them to the Divine protection; adding, "and though I feel them near to me at this time, yet I freely give them up, having a hope that they will be provided for." A little after he said, "This trial is made easier than I could have thought, my will being wholly taken away; for if I was anxious for the event, it would have been harder, but I am not, and my mind enjoys a perfect calm."

In the night a young woman having given him something to drink, he said, "My child, thou seems very kind to me, a poor creature, the Lord will reward thee for it." Awhile after he cried out with great earnestness of spirit, "Oh, my Father! my Father!" and soon after he said, "Oh, my Father! my Father! how comfortable art thou to my soul in this trying season." Being asked if he could take a little nourishment, after some pause he replied, "My child, I cannot tell what to say to it; I seem nearly arrived where my soul shall have rest from all its troubles." After giving in something to be inserted in his Journal, he said, "I believe the Lord will now excuse me from exercises of this kind. I see no work but one, which is to be the last wrought by me in this world; the messenger will come that will release me from all these troubles; but it must be in the Lord's time, which I am waiting for." He said he had labored to do whatever was required, according to the ability received, in the remembrance of which he had peace; and though the disorder was strong at times, and would like a whirlwind come over his mind, yet it had hitherto been kept steady and centred in everlasting love; adding, "and if that be mercifully continued, I ask or desire no more." Another time he said, he had long had a view of visiting this nation, and some time before he came had a dream, in which he saw himself in the northern parts of it, and that the spring of the Gospel was opened in him much as in the beginning of Friends, such as George Fox and William Dewsbury; and he saw the different states of the people as clearly as he had ever seen flowers in a garden; but in his going along he was suddenly stopped, though he could not see for what end; but looking toward home, fell into a flood of tears which waked him.

At another time he said, "My draught seemed strongest toward the North, and I mentioned in my own Monthly Meeting, that attending the Quarterly Meeting at York, and being there looked like home to me."

Fifth-day night, having repeatedly consented to take medicine with a view to settle his stomach, but without effect: the Friend then waiting on him, said through distress, "What shall I do now?" He answered with great composure, "Rejoice evermore, and in everything give thanks," but added a little after, "This is sometimes hard to come at."

Sixth-day morning early, he broke forth in supplication on this wise, "O Lord, it was thy power that enabled me to forsake sin in my youth, and I have felt thy bruises for disobedience, but as I bowed under them thou healed me, continuing a father and a friend. I feel thy power now, and I beg that in the approaching trying moment thou wilt keep my heart steadfast unto thee."—Upon his giving directions to a friend concerning some little things, she said, "I will take care, but hope thou wilt live to order them thyself;" he replied, "My hope is in Christ, and though I may seem a little better, a change in the disorder may soon happen, and my little strength be dissolved, and if it so happen, I shall be gathered to my everlasting rest." On her saying she did not doubt that, but could not help mourning to see so many faithful servants removed at so low a time, he said, "All good cometh from the Lord, whose power is the same, and can work as he sees best." The same day he had given directions about wrapping his corpse; and perceiving a Friend to weep, he said: "I would rather thou wouldst guard against weeping for me, my sister; I sorrow not, though I have had some painful conflicts, but now they seem over and matters well settled, and I look at the face of my dear Redeemer, for sweet is his voice and his countenance is comely."

First-day, 4th of the tenth month, being very weak and in general difficult to be understood, he uttered a few words in commemoration of the Lord's goodness; and added, "How tenderly have I been waited on in this time of affliction, in which I may say in Job's words, 'Tedious days and wearisome nights are appointed unto me'; and how many are spending their time and money in vanity and superfluities, while thousands and tens of thousands want the necessaries of life, who might be relieved by them, and their distresses at such a time as this, in some degree softened by the administering suitable things."

Second-day morning, the apothecary who appeared very anxious to assist him, being present, he queried about the probability of such a load of matter being thrown off his weak body, and the apothecary making some remarks implying that he thought it might; he spoke with an audible voice on this wise, "My dependence is on the Lord Jesus, who I trust will forgive my sins, which is all I hope for, and if it be his will to raise up this body again, I am content; and if to die, I am resigned; and if thou canst not be easy without trying to assist nature, I submit:" after which his throat was so much affected, that it was very difficult for him to speak so as to be understood, and he frequently wrote when he wanted anything. About the second hour on fourth-day morning he asked for pen and ink, and at several times with much difficulty wrote thus, "I believe my being here is in the wisdom of Christ, I know not as to life or death."

About a quarter before six o'clock the same morning he seemed to fall into an easy sleep, which continued about half an hour, when seeming to awake, he breathed a few times with more difficulty, and expired without sigh, groan, or struggle.

NOTES

Page 3. This statement must not be taken as a confession of evil doing, but as an expression of the deep sense of unworthiness which comes to many conscientious and sensitive men and women. A similar statement was made by John Bunyan.

Page 6. The Friends rejected the traditional observance of seasons and days by religious services, with the exception of Sunday, which they called first-day.

Page 7. The word "plantation" has been used in this country chiefly in the Southern States, and usually, though not necessarily, meant a large tract of land. It was used, however, in the earlier history of the country in the same way in which the word "farm" is now used.

Page 8. In the early days of the colonies convicts, and boys and girls who had been kidnapped in England, were brought over and sold for a term of years. A considerable number of very poor people sold themselves for a term of years in order to secure passage to the New World; such persons serving their purchasers until the debt incurred to the ship-owners was cancelled. These "indented servants" were called redemptioners.

Page 10. The Friends did not observe Christmas.

Page 11. Negroes were brought to the colonies and sold as slaves at a very early date, and slavery existed in all the colonies before the Revolution.

Page 12. The Friends, or Quakers, among whom Woolman was a leader, formed a religious society which was organized in England during the last half of the seventeenth century through the influence of the preaching and teaching of George Fox. They rejected all kinds of ecclesiastical organization, all creeds and forms; they believed in the guidance of the inward spirit and in a self-supporting ministry; they were opposed to war; they practised frugality, industry, and thrift; and they separated themselves from other men by peculiarities of dress.

Page 12. The Friends dropped the names of the months and numbered them.

Page 16. In order to secure order and discipline, the Friends, at an early date in their history, adopted the plan of dealing with such matters in certain meetings or assemblies: preparative meetings, monthly meetings, quarterly meetings, and yearly meetings.

Page 20. See note, p. 16.

Page 54. Opposition to war was so much a matter of conscience with many Friends that they allowed their property to be seized by the authorities rather than pay taxes imposed to carry on or defray the expense of war.

Page 56. The Mennonists or Mennonites were followers of Menno, a Dutch priest, who, about 1540, organized the Anabaptists in Holland and Germany into one body; teaching the personal reign of Christ on earth, the unlawfulness of war, of oaths, and of lawsuits. The Mennonites first came to this country in 1683, and were invited by William Penn to settle in the province of Pennsylvania.

Page 59. Thomas à Kempis, a German monk who entered the Augustinian monastery of Utrecht in 1400; a man of great piety and a voluminous writer of hymns, sermons, biographies, and letters, remembered chiefly, however, as the probable author of "The Imitation of Christ," one of the most widely known books in the literature of the world.

Page 59. John Huss, a Bohemian reformer, student in the University of Prague, a preacher of great learning and power, became a follower of Wickliffe and a bold critic of ecclesiastical corruption, was burned at Constance in 1415.

Page 59. Compare Huss's words with the famous declaration of Luther regarding his going to Worms.

Page 63. Fort William Henry, a fortified post on Lake Champlain, N.Y., during the French and Indian War.

Page 116. The Six Nations was a union or confederation of the Oneidas, Mohawks, Onondagas, Cayugas, and Senecas, powerful Indian tribes in Central and Western New York; the Tuscaroras joined the confederation later. The Six Nations numbered about 15,000, each tribe being governed by its own sachems, and the whole body by a council of sachems.

Dana's Two Years before the Mast. Edited by Homer E. Keyes, Dartmouth College.

Defoe's Robinson Crusoe. Edited by Clifton Johnson.

De Quincey's Confessions of an English Opium-Eater. Edited by Arthur Beatty, University of Wisconsin.

De Quincey's Joan of Arc and The English Mail-Coach. Edited by Carol M. Newman, Virginia Polytechnic Institute.

Dickens's A Christmas Carol and The Cricket on the Hearth. Edited by James M. Sawin, with the collaboration of Ida M. Thomas.

Dickens's A Tale of Two Cities. Edited by H. G. Buehler, Hotchkiss School, Lakeville, Conn., and L. Mason.

Dryden's Palamon and Arcite. Edited by Percival Chubb, Vice-Principal Ethical Culture Schools, New York City.

Early American Orations, 1760–1824. Edited by Louie R. Heller, Instructor in English in the De Witt Clinton High School, New York City.

Edwards's (Jonathan) Sermons (Selections). Edited by H. N. Gardiner, Professor of Philosophy, Smith College.

Emerson's Earlier Poems. Edited by O. C. Gallagher.

Emerson's Essays (Selected). Edited by Eugene D. Holmes.

Emerson's Representative Men. Edited by Philo Melvyn Buck, Jr.

English Narrative Poems. Edited by C. M. Fuess and H. N. Sanborn.

Epoch-making Papers in United States History. Edited by M. S. Brown, New York University.

Franklin's Autobiography.

Mrs. Gaskell's Cranford. Edited by Professor Martin W. Sampson, Indiana University.

George Eliot's Silas Marner. Edited by E. L. Gulick, Lawrenceville School, Lawrenceville, N.J.

Goldsmith's The Deserted Village and The Traveller. Edited by Robert N. Whiteford, High School, Peoria, Ill.

Goldsmith's Vicar of Wakefield. Edited by H. W. Boynton, Phillips Academy, Andover, Mass.

Gray's Elegy. Edited by J. H. Castleman.

Grimm's Fairy Tales. Edited by James H. Fassett, Superintendent of Schools, Nashua, N.H.

Hawthorne's Grandfather's Chair. Edited by H. H. Kingsley, Superintendent of Schools, Evanston, Ill.

Hawthorne's The House of the Seven Gables. Edited by Clyde Furst.

Hawthorne's Mosses from an Old Manse. Edited by C. E. Burbank.

Hawthorne's Tanglewood Tales. Edited by R. H. Beggs.

Hawthorne's Twice-Told Tales. Edited by C. R. Gaston.

Hawthorne's The Wonder-Book. Edited by L. E. Wolfe, Superintendent of Schools, San Antonio, Texas.

Homer's Iliad. Translated by Lang, Leaf, and Myers.

Homer's Odyssey. Translated by Butcher and Lang.

Hughes' Tom Brown's School Days. Edited by Charles S. Thomas.

Irving's Alhambra. Edited by Alfred M. Hitchcock, Public High School, Hartford, Conn.

Irving's Knickerbocker History of New York. Edited by Prof. E. A. Greenlaw, Adelphi College, New York City.

Irving's Life of Goldsmith. Edited by GILBERT SYKES BLAKELY, Teacher of English in the Morris High School, New York City.
Irving's Sketch Book.
Keary's Heroes of Asgard. Edited by CHARLES H. MORSS.
Kingsley's The Heroes: Greek Fairy Tales. Edited by CHARLES A. MCMURRY, Ph.D.
Lamb's Essays of Elia. Edited by HELEN J. ROBINS.
Lamb's Tales from Shakespeare. Edited by A. AINGER.
Longfellow's Courtship of Miles Standish. Edited by HOMER P. LEWIS.
Longfellow's Courtship of Miles Standish, and Minor Poems. Edited by W. D. HOWE, Butler College, Indianapolis, Ind.
Longfellow's Evangeline. Edited by LEWIS B. SEMPLE, Commercial High School, Brooklyn, N.Y.
Longfellow's Tales of a Wayside Inn. Edited by J. H. CASTLEMAN.
Longfellow's The Song of Hiawatha. Edited by ELIZABETH J. FLEMING, Teachers' Training School, Baltimore, Md.
Lowell's Vision of Sir Launfal. Edited by HERBERT E. BATES, Manual Training High School, Brooklyn, N.Y.
Macaulay's Essay on Addison. Edited by C. W. FRENCH, Principal of Hyde Park High School, Chicago, Ill.
Macaulay's Essay on Clive. Edited by J. W. PEARCE, Assistant Professor of English in Tulane University.
Macaulay's Essay on Johnson. Edited by WILLIAM SCHUYLER, Assistant Principal of the St. Louis High School.
Macaulay's Essay on Milton. Edited by C. W. FRENCH.
Macaulay's Essay on Warren Hastings. Edited by Mrs. M. J. FRICK, Los Angeles, Cal.
Macaulay's Lays of Ancient Rome, and other Poems. Edited by FRANKLIN T. BAKER, Teachers College, Columbia University.
Malory's Morte d'Arthur (Selections). Edited by D. W. SWIGGETT.
Memorable Passages from the Bible (Authorized Version). Selected and edited by FRED NEWTON SCOTT, Professor of Rhetoric in the University of Michigan.
Milton's Comus, Lycidas, and other Poems. Edited by ANDREW J. GEORGE.
Milton's Paradise Lost, Books I and II. Edited by W. I. CRANE.
Old English Ballads. Edited by WILLIAM D. ARMES, of the University of California.
Out of the Northland. Edited by EMILIE KIP BAKER.
Palgrave's Golden Treasury of Songs and Lyrics.
Plutarch's Lives of Cæsar, Brutus, and Antony. Edited by MARTHA BRIER, Polytechnic High School, Oakland, Cal.
Poe's Poems. Edited by CHARLES W. KENT, University of Virginia.
Poe's Prose Tales (Selections from).
Pope's Homer's Iliad. Edited by ALBERT SMYTH, Head Professor of English Language and Literature, Central High School, Philadelphia, Pa.
Pope's The Rape of the Lock. Edited by ELIZABETH M. KING.
Ruskin's Sesame and Lilies and The King of the Golden River. Edited by HERBERT E. BATES.
Scott's Ivanhoe. Edited by ALFRED M. HITCHCOCK.
Scott's Kenilworth. Edited by J. H. CASTLEMAN.

Scott's Lady of the Lake. Edited by ELIZABETH A. PACKARD.
Scott's Lay of the Last Minstrel. Edited by RALPH H. BOWLES.
Scott's Marmion. Edited by GEORGE B. AITON, State Inspector of High Schools for Minnesota.
Scott's Quentin Durward. Edited by ARTHUR LLEWELLYN ENO, Instructor in the University of Illinois.
Scott's The Talisman. Edited by FREDERICK TREUDLEY, State Normal College, Ohio University.
Shakespeare's As You Like It. Edited by CHARLES ROBERT GASTON.
Shakespeare's Hamlet. Edited by L. A. SHERMAN, Professor of English Literature in the University of Nebraska.
Shakespeare's Henry V. Edited by RALPH HARTT BOWLES, Phillips Exeter Academy, Exeter, N.H.
Shakespeare's Julius Cæsar. Edited by GEORGE W. HUFFORD and LOIS G. HUFFORD, High School, Indianapolis, Ind.
Shakespeare's Macbeth. Edited by C. W. FRENCH.
Shakespeare's Merchant of Venice. Edited by CHARLOTTE W. UNDERWOOD, Lewis Institute, Chicago, Ill.
Shakespeare's Midsummer Night's Dream. Edited by E. C. NOYES.
Shakespeare's Richard II. Edited by JAMES HUGH MOFFATT.
Shakespeare's The Tempest. Edited by S. C. NEWSOM.
Shakespeare's Twelfth Night. Edited by EDWARD P. MORTON.
Shelley and Keats (Selections from). Edited by S. C. NEWSOM.
Sheridan's The Rivals, and The School for Scandal. Edited by W. D. HOWE.
Southern Poets (Selections from). Edited by W. L. WEBER.
Spenser's Faerie Queene, Book I. Edited by GEORGE ARMSTRONG WAUCHOPE, Professor of English in the South Carolina College.
Stevenson's Kidnapped. Edited by JOHN THOMPSON BROWN.
Stevenson's Master of Ballantrae. Edited by H. A. WHITE.
Stevenson's Treasure Island. Edited by H. A. VANCE, Professor of English in the University of Nashville.
Swift's Gulliver's Travels. Edited by CLIFTON JOHNSON.
Tennyson's Idylls of the King. Edited by W. T. VLYMEN, Principal of Eastern District High School, Brooklyn, N.Y.
Tennyson's Shorter Poems. Edited by CHARLES READ NUTTER.
Tennyson's The Princess. Edited by WILSON FARRAND.
Thackeray's Henry Esmond. Edited by JOHN BELL HENNEMAN, University of the South, Sewanee, Tenn.
Washington's Farewell Address, and Webster's First Bunker Hill Oration. Edited by WILLIAM T. PECK.
John Woolman's Journal.
Wordsworth's Shorter Poems. Edited by EDWARD FULTON.

THE MACMILLAN COMPANY

64–66 FIFTH AVENUE, NEW YORK